CROCK·POT®

◆ THE ORIGINAL SLOW COOKER ◆

Gourmet
Slow Cooking

WEST
SIDE
PUBLISHING

Recipes on pages 10, 12, 20, 21, 38, 68, 78, 150, 202, 204 and 226 developed by Amy Golino.
Front cover photography and photography on pages 9, 11, 13, 15, 17, 19, 25, 39, 61, 63, 65, 67, 69, 71, 73, 75, 77, 79, 95, 97, 99, 101, 103, 105, 107, 109, 111, 113, 115, 117, 119, 121, 123, 125, 127, 129, 131, 133, 135, 137, 139, 143, 151, 157, 163, 165, 167, 171, 197, 205, 215, 217, 219 and 227 by Stephen Hamilton Photographics, Ltd.

Pictured on the front cover: Asian Beef with Mandarin Oranges *(page 134)*.
Pictured on the inside front cover: Gingerbread *(page 230)*.
Pictured on the back cover (clockwise from top): Orange-Date Nut Bread *(page 32)*, Braised Sea Bass with Aromatic Vegetables *(page 78)* and Ham & Sage-Stuffed Cornish Hens *(page 60)*.
Pictured on the inside back cover (from top): Mucho Mocha Cocoa *(page 196)*, Spiked Sponge Cake *(page 244)* and Tequila-Poached Pears *(page 216)*.

ISBN-13: 978-1-4127-9936-2
ISBN-10: 1-4127-9936-8

Manufactured in China.

8 7 6 5 4 3 2 1

Microwave Cooking: Microwave ovens vary in wattage. Use the cooking times as guidelines and check for doneness before adding more time.

Preparation/Cooking Times: Preparation times are based on the approximate amount of time required to assemble the recipe before cooking, baking, chilling or serving. These times include preparation steps such as measuring, chopping and mixing. The fact that some preparations and cooking can be done simultaneously is taken into account. Preparation of optional ingredients and serving suggestions is not included.

Contents

108

26

214

Gourmet the Slow Cooker Way

Sure, you know how to use your **CROCK-POT®** slow cooker to turn out perfectly respectable meals with a minimum of hassle. You keep your family well-fed, so you're happy, even if you're basically choosing recipes out of habit.

Tired of cooking the same meals? Need to mix it up, experiment a little? Want to find a way to apply time-saving cooking techniques to weeknight suppers and entertaining menus?

Help is here! The book you're holding now showcases recipes for the adventurous home cook. Inside you'll find exciting and exotic flavors and techniques that take cooking with a **CROCK-POT®** slow cooker to a new level.

What's more, these recipes are as simple to put together as the classic dishes your family already loves. Even better, all of the ingredients can be found in American supermarkets. Recipes like Thai Coconut Chicken Meatballs (page 96) or Duck Confit and Mushroom Salad (page 68) are sure to get your next party started right, while

being just as simple to prepare as your favorite mac and cheese recipe. You'll even find an entire chapter of beverage recipes like Mucho Mocha Cocoa (page 196) and Infused Mint Mojitos (page 204).

But this book contains more than just new ideas for fancy party foods. Check out breakfast and brunch ideas like Apple-Cinnamon Breakfast Risotto (page 52) or Chocolate-Stuffed Slow Cooker French Toast (page 46) fun enough for company but so good you'll find reasons to make them for yourself.

More importantly you'll find plenty of recipes, like Braised Sea Bass with Aromatic Vegetables (page 78) or Saffron-Scented Paella (page 141), that are perfect to serve as main dishes or sides any night of the week.

Slow Cooker Tips and Techniques

Slow Cooker Sizes

Smaller slow cookers, such as 1-quart to 3½-quart models, are the perfect size for singles, a couple, empty-nesters and also for serving dips.

While medium size slow cookers (those holding somewhere between 3 quarts and 5 quarts) will easily cook enough food at a time to feed a small family, these sizes are also convenient for holiday side dishes or appetizers.

Large slow cookers are great for large family dinners, holiday entertaining and potluck suppers. A 6- to 7-quart model is ideal if you like to make meals in advance and have dinner tonight and store leftovers for another day.

Types of Slow Cookers

Current models of **CROCK-POT**® slow cookers come equipped with many different features and benefits, from auto cook programs, to stovetop-safe stoneware to timed programming. Visit www.crockpot.com to find the slow cooker that best suits your needs and lifestyle.

Cooking, Stirring and Food Safety

CROCK-POT® slow cookers are safe to leave unattended. The outer heating base may get hot as it cooks, but it should not pose a fire hazard. The heating element in the heating base functions at a low wattage and is safe for most countertops.

Your slow cooker should be filled about ½ to ¾ for most recipes unless otherwise instructed. Lean meats such as chicken or pork tenderloin will cook faster than meats with more connective tissue and fat such as beef chuck or pork shoulder. Bone-in meats will take longer than boneless cuts. Typical slow cooker dishes take approximately 7 to 8 hours to reach the simmer point on LOW and about 3 to 4 hours on HIGH. Once the vegetables and meat start to simmer and braise, their flavors will fully blend and meat will become fall-off-the bone tender.

According to the USDA, all bacteria are killed at a temperature of 165° F. It is important to follow the recommended cooking times and to keep the lid closed, especially early in the cooking process when heat is building up inside the unit. If you need to open the lid to check on your food or are adding additional ingredients, remember to allow additional cooking time if necessary to ensure food is cooked through and tender.

Large slow cookers, the 6- to 7-quart sizes, may benefit with a quick stir halfway during cook time to help distribute heat and promote even cooking. It is usually unnecessary to stir at all as even ½ cup liquid will help to distribute heat and the crockery is the perfect medium for holding food at an even temperature throughout the cooking process.

Oven-Safe

All **CROCK-POT**® slow cooker removable crockery inserts may (without their lids) be used in ovens at up to 400°F. Also, all **CROCK-POT**® slow cooker crockery inserts are microwavable without their lids. If you own another brand slow cooker, please refer to your owner's manual for specific crockery cooking medium tolerances.

Frozen Food

Frozen food or partially frozen food can be successfully cooked in a slow cooker, however it will require longer cooking than the same recipe made with fresh food. Using an instant read thermometer is recommended to ensure meat is fully cooked through.

Pasta and Rice

If you are converting a recipe that calls for uncooked pasta, cook them on the stovetop just until slightly tender before adding to slow cooker. If you are converting a recipe that calls for cooked rice, stir in raw rice with other ingredients; add ¼ cup extra liquid per ¼ cup of raw rice.

Beans

Beans must be softened completely before combining with sugar and/or acidic foods. Sugar and acid have a hardening effect on beans and will prevent softening. Fully cooked canned beans may be used as a substitute for dried beans.

Vegetables

Root vegetables often cook more slowly than meat. Cut vegetables accordingly to cook at the same rate as meat, large or small, or lean versus marbled, and place near the sides or bottom of the stoneware to facilitate cooking.

Herbs

Fresh herbs add flavor and color when added at the end of the cooking cycle but for dishes with shorter cook times, hearty, fresh herbs such as rosemary and thyme hold up well. If added at the beginning, many fresh herbs' flavor will dissipate over long cook times. Ground and/or dried herbs and spices work well in slow cooking and may be added at beginning. The flavor power of all herbs and spices can vary greatly depending on their particular strength and shelf life. Use chili powders and garlic powder sparingly as these can sometimes intensify over the long cook times. Always taste dish at end of cook cycle and correct seasonings including salt and pepper.

Liquids

It is not necessary to use more than ½ to 1 cup liquid in most instances since juices in meats and vegetables are retained more in slow cooking than in conventional cooking. Excess liquid can be cooked down and concentrated after slow cooking on the stovetop or by removing meat and vegetables from stoneware, stirring in cornstarch or tapioca and setting the slow cooker to HIGH. Cook on HIGH for approximately 15 minutes until juices are thickened.

Milk

Milk, cream, and sour cream break down during extended cooking. When possible, add during last 15 to 30 minutes of cooking, until just heated through. Condensed soups may be substituted for milk and can cook for extended times.

Fish

Fish is delicate and should be stirred in gently during the last 15-30 minutes of cooking time. Cook until just cooked through and serve immediately.

Basic Stocks, Superior Sauces

celery-leek bisque with basil

SERVINGS: 4 TO 6 | PREP TIME: 45 MINUTES
HIGH: 4 HOURS | LOW: 8 HOURS

3 bunches leeks (3 pounds before trimming), trimmed and well rinsed*

2 medium celery stalks, sliced

1 medium carrot, peeled and sliced (3 ounces)

3 cloves garlic, minced

2 cans (14 ounces each) 99% fat-free chicken broth

1 cup cream cheese with garlic and herbs

2 cups half-and-half, plus more for garnish

Salt and black pepper

Fresh basil leaves (optional)

Combine leeks, celery, carrot, garlic and broth in 3½- to 4-quart **CROCK-POT®** slow cooker. Cover and cook on LOW 8 hours or on HIGH 4 hours.

Purée until smooth in blender 1 cup at a time, returning batches to **CROCK-POT®** slow cooker as they are processed. Add cream cheese to last batch in blender and purée until smooth. Stir into soup along with half-and-half. Add salt and pepper to taste. Flavors intensify overnight, so cool to room temperature and then refrigerate in airtight container. Reheat before serving. Garnish with swirl of half-and-half and fresh basil.

TIP: Thoroughly rinsing the leeks is very important. The gritty sand can become trapped between the layers of the leeks and can be difficult to see, therefore several rinsings are imperative to ensure they are completely clean.

pumpkin soup with crumbled bacon & toasted pumpkin seeds

SERVINGS: 4 TO 6 | PREP TIME: 20 MINUTES
HIGH: 4 HOURS

2	teaspoons olive oil
½	cup raw pumpkin seeds
3	slices thick-sliced bacon
1	medium onion, chopped
1	teaspoon kosher salt
½	teaspoon chopped dried chipotle pepper, or more to taste
½	teaspoon black pepper
2	cans (29 ounces each) 100% pumpkin purée
4	cups chicken stock or broth
¾	cup apple cider
½	cup heavy cream
	Sour cream (optional)

Coat 3½-quart **CROCK-POT®** slow cooker with nonstick cooking spray.

Heat olive oil in medium skillet over medium heat. Add pumpkin seeds and stir until seeds begin to pop, about 1 minute. Transfer to small bowl and set aside.

Return skillet to heat and add bacon. Cook until crisp, then cool on paper towels. When cool, crumble and set aside.

Meanwhile, return skillet to heat. Add onion and cook, stirring frequently, until translucent. Stir in salt, chipotle pepper and black pepper. Transfer to prepared **CROCK-POT®** slow cooker. Whisk in pumpkin, chicken stock and apple cider and stir until smooth. Cover and cook on HIGH 4 hours.

Turn CROCK-POT® slow cooker off and remove lid. Whisk in heavy cream. Season to taste with additional salt and pepper. Strain and keep warm until serving. To serve, ladle into soup bowls and garnish with sour cream, toasted pumpkin seeds and crumbled bacon.

TIP: Pumpkin seeds (or "pepitas") are a common ingredient in Mexican cooking. They can be purchased raw or roasted and salted; either variety may be found hulled or whole.

greek lemon & rice soup

SERVINGS: 4 | PREP TIME: 20 MINUTES
HIGH: 2 TO 3 HOURS

3   cans (14 ounces each) chicken broth

½   cup uncooked long-grain rice

3   egg yolks

¼   cup fresh lemon juice

     Salt and black pepper

4   thin slices lemon (optional)

4   teaspoons finely chopped fresh parsley (optional)

Stir together chicken broth and rice in 4-quart **CROCK-POT®** slow cooker. Cover and cook on HIGH 2 to 3 hours or until rice is tender and fully cooked.

When rice is cooked turn **CROCK-POT®** slow cooker to LOW. Whisk together egg yolks and lemon juice in medium bowl. Add large spoonful of hot rice mixture to egg yolk mixture and whisk together briefly, then whisk this mixture back into remaining rice mixture. Cover and cook on LOW setting 10 minutes longer.

Season to taste with salt and pepper. Ladle into bowls; garnish each bowl with 1 lemon slice and sprinkle with chopped parsley. Soup may be served hot or cold. To serve soup cold, cool to room temperature. Cover and refrigerate up to 24 hours before serving.

slow cooker chicken stock

SERVINGS: ABOUT 4½ TO 5 QUARTS | PREP TIME: 1 HOUR
HIGH: 8 HOURS | LOW: 12 HOURS

1   chicken (4 to 6 pounds), cut into 8 pieces

1   pound celery, cut into large pieces

1   large carrot, peeled and cut into large chunks

2   onions, quartered

2   large parsnips, peeled and coarsely chopped

½   cup loosely packed fresh herbs such as flat-leaf parsley, dill, thyme, chervil or combination

     Kosher salt and black pepper

Place all ingredients except salt and pepper in 6- to 7-quart **CROCK-POT®** slow cooker. Add enough water to fill three-fourths full. Cover and cook on LOW 12 hours or on HIGH 8 hours.

Strain out solids and season to taste with salt and pepper. Cool to room temperature, then cover and refrigerate 12 hours. Remove any fat congealed on top of stock before using.

greek lemon & rice soup

french lentil rice soup

SERVINGS: 4 | PREP TIME: 30 MINUTES
HIGH: 4 TO 5 HOURS | LOW: 8 HOURS

6   cups chicken or vegetable broth

1   cup dried lentils, rinsed and picked over

2   medium carrots, peeled and finely diced

1   small onion, finely chopped

2   stalks celery, finely diced

3   tablespoons uncooked rice

2   teaspoons minced garlic

1   teaspoon dried herbes de Provence

½   teaspoon salt

⅛   teaspoon ground black pepper

4   tablespoons heavy cream or sour cream

¼   cup chopped fresh parsley

Stir together broth, lentils, carrots, onion, celery, rice, garlic, herbes de Provence, salt and pepper in 5-quart **CROCK-POT®** slow cooker. Cover and cook on LOW 8 hours or on HIGH 4 to 5 hours.

Remove about 1½ cups of soup and purée in food processor or blender until almost smooth. Stir back into remaining soup. To serve, ladle soup into bowls and top each with spoonful of cream and sprinkle with parsley.

shrimp & pepper bisque

SERVINGS: 4 | PREP TIME: 20 MINUTES
HIGH: 4 HOURS | LOW: 8 HOURS

1   bag (12 ounces) frozen stir-fry-style mixed peppers and vegetables, thawed

½   pound frozen cauliflower florettes, thawed

1   medium stalk celery, sliced

1   can (14½ ounces) 99% fat-free chicken broth

1   tablespoon seafood seasoning

½   teaspoon dried thyme

12   ounces raw medium shrimp, peeled

2   cups half-and-half

2   to 3 green onions, green and white parts, finely chopped

Combine thawed stir-fry mix, cauliflower, celery, chicken broth, seafood seasoning and thyme in 3½- to 4-quart **CROCK-POT®** slow cooker. Cover and cook on LOW 8 hours or on HIGH 4 hours.

Stir in shrimp and cook, covered, 15 minutes or until no longer pink in center. Purée until smooth in blender 1 cup at a time, returning batches to **CROCK-POT®** slow cooker. Stir in half-and-half. To serve, ladle into bowls and sprinkle with chopped green onions.

TIP: For a creamier, smoother consistency strain through several layers of damp cheesecloth.

creamy sweet potato & butternut squash soup

SERVINGS: 4 TO 6 | PREP TIME: 20 MINUTES
HIGH: 4 HOURS

1   **pound sweet potatoes, peeled and cut into 1-inch cubes (about 3 cups total)**

1   **pound butternut squash, peeled and diced into 1-inch cubes (about 3½ cups total)**

½   **cup chopped onion**

1   **can (14 ounces) chicken broth, divided**

½   **cup (1 stick) butter, diced**

1   **can (13½ ounces) coconut milk**

½   **teaspoon ground cumin**

½   **teaspoon ground red pepper, or more to taste**

1½   **teaspoons salt, or more to taste**

3   **to 4 green onions, green and white parts, finely chopped (optional)**

Combine sweet potatoes, squash, onion, half of chicken broth and butter in 4½-quart **CROCK-POT®** slow cooker. Cover and cook on HIGH 4 hours or until vegetables are tender.

Purée until smooth in blender 1 cup at a time, returning batches to **CROCK-POT®** slow cooker. Stir in remaining broth, coconut milk, ground cumin, ground red pepper and salt. To serve, ladle into bowls and sprinkle with chopped green onions.

slow cooker beef or veal stock

SERVINGS: 2½ TO 3 QUARTS | PREP TIME: 45 MINUTES
HIGH: 7 TO 8 HOURS | LOW: 10 TO 12 HOURS

3	to 4 pounds marrow or knuckle veal bones
2	quarts plus 1 cup water, divided
2	large leeks, thoroughly cleaned, cut into 1-inch pieces
3	carrots, cut into 1-inch pieces
3	cups coarsely chopped onions
2	stalks celery, cut into 1-inch pieces
1	tablespoon tomato paste
2	sprigs fresh thyme
2	large sprigs fresh flat-leaf parsley
1	bay leaf
½	tablespoon black peppercorns

Preheat oven to 450°F. Arrange veal bones in single layer in large roasting pan and roast in middle of oven, turning once or twice, until browned, 30 to 45 minutes.

Transfer bones to 6- to 7-quart **CROCK-POT®** slow cooker with 2 quarts water over bones.

Discard fat from roasting pan. Pour ½ cup water into roasting pan then stir with wooden spoon to scrape up brown bits; pour over bones. Cover and cook on LOW 8 to 10 hours on HIGH 5 to 6 hours.

With 20 to 30 minutes left in bones' cooking time, oil clean roasting pan and add leeks, carrots, onions and celery in single layer. Roast in middle of preheated 450°F oven, stirring once or twice, until golden brown, 20 to 30 minutes. Transfer vegetables to **CROCK-POT®** slow cooker and immediately add remaining ½ cup water to hot pan, stirring to scrape up brown bits, then add to **CROCK-POT®** slow cooker. Stir in thyme, parsley, bay leaf and peppercorns. Cover and cook on HIGH 2 hours.

Remove bones with tongs and discard. Pour stock in batches through a large sieve into large pot or Dutch oven and discard strained solids. Allow stock to cool to room temperature and place in refrigerator overnight. Before using or freezing, remove congealed fat from chilled stock.

TIP: To quickly cool down stock for safe refrigerator storage, pour strained stock into a large pot or Dutch oven and place in a sinkful or large bowlful of ice, stirring often.

slow cooker vegetable stock

SERVINGS: ABOUT 4½ TO 5 QUARTS | PREP TIME: 35 MINUTES
HIGH: 6 TO 8 HOURS | LOW: 10 TO 12 HOURS

3 carrots, coarsely chopped

3 parsnips, coarsely chopped

3 onions, quartered

3 leeks, coarsely chopped

3 stalks celery, coarsely chopped

3 bay leaves

2 sprigs fresh thyme

4 sprigs fresh parsley

8 whole peppercorns

   Water

   Kosher salt, to taste

Combine all ingredients except salt in 6- to 7-quart **CROCK-POT®** slow cooker. Fill three-fourths full with water. Season with salt. Cook on LOW 10 to 12 hours or on HIGH 6 to 8 hours.

Strain stock and discard solids. Cool to room temperature and refrigerate, freeze or use immediately.

Cook's Tip: Varying the vegetables to suit the soup offers limitless possibilities with additions such as turnip, sweet potato, yam, rutabaga, celery root, fennel or mushrooms.

TIP: Herbs and spices or combination thereof can be used to create many different flavors of stock made from the same list of basic ingredients. Try classic herbs and spices such bay leaf, thyme, rosemary, parsley and chives. Also be sure to experiment with more exotic flavors such as Thai basil, mint, cilantro, ginger, lemongrass and star anise, and with sauces like nam pla, oyster sauce or soy sauce.

spaghetti sauce

SERVINGS: 6 | PREP TIME: 15 MINUTES
LOW: 6 TO 8 HOURS

1	tablespoon olive oil
1½	pounds ground beef
1	medium onion, chopped
1	medium green bell pepper, diced
2	cans (28 ounces each) crushed tomatoes, undrained
2	cups beef stock (see recipe page 20)
1	can (8 ounces) tomato sauce
1	can (6 ounces) tomato paste (or more to taste)
½	cup grated Parmesan cheese
1	tablespoon brown sugar
2	teaspoons garlic powder
1	teaspoon dried oregano
1	teaspoon dried basil

Heat oil in large skillet over medium-low heat. Add ground beef, onion and bell pepper. Cook, stirring frequently, until meat is no longer pink and onion is tender. Drain excess fat.

Transfer meat mixture to 4½-quart **CROCK-POT®** slow cooker. Add remaining ingredients; stir thoroughly. Cover; cook on LOW 6 to 8 hours.

roasted tomato-basil soup

SERVINGS: 6 | PREP TIME: 10 MINUTES
HIGH: 4½ HOURS | LOW: 8½ HOURS

2 cans (28 ounces each) whole tomatoes, drained and juice reserved (about 3 cups juice)

2½ tablespoons packed dark brown sugar

1 medium onion, finely chopped

3 cups chicken stock (see recipe on page 12)

3 tablespoons tomato paste

¼ teaspoon ground allspice

1 can (5 ounces) evaporated milk

¼ cup chopped fresh basil

Salt and black pepper

Additional fresh basil (optional)

Onion slices (optional)

Preheat oven to 450°F. Line baking sheet with foil; spray with nonstick cooking spray. Arrange tomatoes on foil in single layer. Sprinkle with brown sugar; top with onion. Bake 25 to 30 minutes or until tomatoes look dry and are lightly browned. Let tomatoes cool slightly; chop finely.

Place tomato mixture, 3 cups reserved juice from tomatoes, chicken broth, tomato paste and allspice in 4½-quart **CROCK-POT®** slow cooker; mix well. Cover; cook on LOW 8 hours or on HIGH 4 hours.

Add evaporated milk and basil; season with salt and pepper. Cook on HIGH 30 minutes or until hot. Garnish with basil and onion slices.

caramelized onion sauce

SERVINGS: ABOUT 3 CUPS | PREP TIME: 35 MINUTES
LOW: 8 TO 10 HOURS

½ cup (1 stick) butter, cut into pieces

3 pounds onions

2 teaspoons balsamic vinegar

1 teaspoon salt

½ teaspoon black pepper

½ cup beef stock (see recipe on page 20)

Coat 3½-quart **CROCK-POT®** slow cooker with nonstick cooking spray. Place butter in **CROCK-POT®** slow cooker. Cover and cook on HIGH to melt.

Meanwhile, slice onions in half through stem ends. Remove outer peels and place flat on cutting surface. Slice onions thinly, holding knife at an angle, cutting through to center. Add to melted butter. Stir in vinegar, salt and pepper. Turn to LOW, do NOT cover and cook for 8 to 10 hours or until onions are brown, soft and reduced in volume to about 3 cups.

Stir in beef stock, scraping bottom and sides with wooden spoon to stir up any bits of browned onions stuck to **CROCK-POT®** slow cooker. Serve immediately or cool to room temperature and refrigerate in airtight container until needed. Reheat before serving.

Serving Suggestion: This onion sauce is fabulous served over your favorite roasted poultry or meat.

TIP: For a thicker sauce, after adding beef stock turn to HIGH and cook to desired consistency.

Daybreak Delights

hawaiian fruit compote

SERVINGS: 6 TO 8 | PREP TIME: 15 MINUTES
HIGH: 2 TO 3 HOURS | LOW: 4 TO 5 HOURS

3 cups coarsely chopped fresh pineapple

3 grapefruits, peeled and sectioned

2 cups chopped fresh peaches

2 to 3 limes, peeled and sectioned

1 mango, peeled and chopped

2 bananas, peeled and sliced

1 tablespoon lemon juice

1 can (21 ounces) cherry pie filling

Slivered almonds (optional)

Place all ingredients, except almonds, in 4½-quart **CROCK-POT®** slow cooker and toss lightly. Cover; cook on LOW 4 to 5 hours or on HIGH 2 to 3 hours.

Serve with almonds, if desired.

Serving Suggestion: Try warm, fruity compote in place of maple syrup on your favorite pancakes or waffles for a great way to start your day. This sauce is also delicious served over roasted turkey, pork roast or baked ham.

breakfast berry bread pudding

6 cups bread, preferably dense peasant-style or sourdough, cut into ¾- to 1-inch cubes

½ cup slivered almonds, toasted*

1 cup raisins

6 large eggs, beaten

1¾ cup milk

1 teaspoon vanilla

1½ cups packed light brown sugar

1½ teaspoons cinnamon

3 cups sliced fresh strawberries

2 cups fresh blueberries

Fresh mint leaves (optional)

*To toast almonds, spread in single layer in heavy-bottomed skillet. Cook over medium heat 1 to 2 minutes, stirring frequently, until nuts are lightly browned. Remove from skillet immediately. Cool before using.

Coat 4½-quart **CROCK-POT**® slow cooker with nonstick cooking spray or butter. Add bread, almonds and raisins, and toss to combine.

Whisk together eggs, milk, vanilla, brown sugar and cinnamon in separate bowl. Pour egg mixture over bread mixture; toss to blend. Cover; cook on LOW 4 to 4½ hours or on HIGH 3 hours.

Remove stoneware from **CROCK-POT**® base and allow bread pudding to cool and set before serving. Serve with berries and garnish with mint leaves, if desired.

oatmeal crème brûlée

SERVINGS: 4 TO 6 | PREP TIME: 15 MINUTES

LOW: 3½ TO 3¾ HOURS

4	cups boiling water
3	cups quick-cooking oatmeal
½	teaspoon salt
6	egg yolks
½	cup granulated sugar
2	cups whipping cream
1	teaspoon vanilla
¼	cup packed light brown sugar
	Fresh berries (optional)

Coat 4½-quart **CROCK-POT**® slow cooker with nonstick cooking spray. Pour in boiling water; stir in oatmeal and salt. Cover and cook on HIGH while making custard.

Combine egg yolks and granulated sugar in small bowl. Mix well; set aside. Heat cream and vanilla in medium saucepan over medium heat until mixture begins to simmer (do not boil). Remove from heat. Whisk ½ cup hot cream into yolks, stirring rapidly so yolks don't cook.* Whisk warmed egg mixture into cream, stirring rapidly to blend well. Spoon mixture over oatmeal. Do not stir.

Turn CROCK-POT® slow cooker to LOW. Line lid with 2 paper towels. Cover tightly; cook on LOW 3 to 3½ hours or until custard has set.

Uncover and sprinkle brown sugar over surface of custard. Line lid with 2 dry paper towels. Cover tightly; continue cooking on LOW 10 to 15 minutes or until brown sugar has melted. Serve with fresh berries, if desired.

Place bowl on damp towel to prevent slipping.

orange date-nut bread

SERVINGS: 8 TO 10 | PREP TIME: 25 MINUTES

HIGH: 2½ HOURS

2   cups unbleached all-purpose flour

½   cup chopped pecans

1   teaspoon baking powder

½   teaspoon baking soda

¼   teaspoon salt

1   cup chopped dates

2   teaspoons dried orange peel

⅔   cup boiling water

¾   cup sugar

2   tablespoons shortening

1   egg, lightly beaten

1   teaspoon vanilla

Spray 1-quart casserole, soufflé dish or other high-sided baking pan with nonstick cooking spray; dust with flour. Set aside.

Combine flour, pecans, baking powder, baking soda and salt in medium bowl; set aside.

Combine dates and orange peel in separate medium bowl; pour boiling water over date mixture. Add sugar, shortening, egg and vanilla; stir just until blended.

Add flour mixture to date mixture; stir just until blended. Pour batter into prepared dish; place in 4½-quart **CROCK-POT®** slow cooker. Cover; cook on HIGH about 2½ hours or until edges begin to brown.

Remove dish. Cool on wire rack about 10 minutes; remove bread from dish and cool completely on rack.

Variation: Substitute 1 cup dried cranberries for dates.

wake-up potato & sausage breakfast casserole

SERVINGS: 8 | PREP TIME: 15 MINUTES

LOW: 6 TO 7 HOURS

1 pound kielbasa or smoked sausage, diced

1 cup chopped onion

1 cup chopped red bell pepper

1 package (20 ounces) refrigerated Southwestern-style hash browns*

10 large eggs

1 cup milk

1 cup shredded Monterey Jack or sharp Cheddar cheese

*If unavailable, you may substitute O'Brien potatoes and add ½ teaspoon chili pepper.

Coat 4½-quart **CROCK-POT®** slow cooker with nonstick cooking spray. Heat large skillet over medium-high heat until hot. Add sausage and onion. Cook and stir until sausage is browned. Drain and discard excess fat. Stir in bell pepper.

Place one-third of potatoes in **CROCK-POT®** slow cooker. Top with one-half of sausage mixture. Repeat layers. Spread remaining one-third of potatoes evenly on top.

Whisk eggs and milk in medium bowl. Pour evenly over potatoes. Cover; cook on LOW 6 to 7 hours.

Turn off **CROCK-POT®** slow cooker. Sprinkle on cheese, and let stand 10 minutes or until cheese is melted. To serve, spoon onto plates.

TIP: For an attractive presentation on a buffet table, turn casserole out onto serving platter. Run a rubber spatula around the outer edges, lifting the bottom slightly. Invert onto a plate. Place a serving plate on top and invert again. Sprinkle with cheese and let stand until cheese is melted. To serve, cut into wedges.

apple & granola breakfast cobbler

SERVINGS: 4 | PREP TIME: 5 MINUTES
HIGH: 2 TO 3 HOURS | LOW: 6 HOURS

4   Granny Smith apples, peeled, cored and sliced

½   cup packed light brown sugar

1   teaspoon ground cinnamon

1   tablespoon lemon juice

2   tablespoons butter, cut into small pieces

2   cups granola cereal, plus additional for garnish

Cream, half-and-half or vanilla yogurt (optional)

Place apples in 4½-quart **CROCK-POT®** slow cooker. Sprinkle brown sugar, cinnamon and lemon juice over apples. Stir in butter and granola.

Cover; cook on LOW 6 hours or on HIGH 2 to 3 hours. Serve hot with additional granola sprinkled on top. Serve with cream, if desired.

eggs benedict

SERVINGS: 4 | PREP TIME: 30 MINUTES
HIGH: 3 HOURS

Boiling water

2   teaspoons white vinegar

8   eggs

4   English muffins

8   pieces Canadian bacon

Hollandaise Sauce (recipe follows), warm

Kosher salt and ground black pepper

Chopped chives or flat-leaf parsley (optional)

Fill 6-quart **CROCK-POT®** slow cooker with water 1½ inches deep. Stir in vinegar. Cook on HIGH while preparing ingredients for next step.

Crack eggs, one at a time, into a small bowl and pour into water gently. Cook about 5 minutes or until white is just set and yolks are still soft. Poached eggs may be served immediately, or turn **CROCK-POT®** slow cooker to WARM and add enough cool water to lower temperature to room temperature. Eggs may be held at optimum temperature until serving.

Meanwhile split and toast English muffins to desired doneness. Fry Canadian bacon in large skillet over medium-high heat until golden brown around edges or to desired donenesss.

Place each muffin on separate plate; top each half muffin with 1 slice Canadian Bacon, 1 poached egg and top with Hollandaise sauce. Spinkle with salt and pepper to taste and garnish with chopped chives, if desired.

hollandaise sauce

3   egg yolks

½   teaspoon kosher salt

½   teaspoon ground black pepper*

1   tablespoon cream

1   cup (2 sticks) butter, melted and kept hot

1   tablespoon lemon juice

*For an extra kick of flavor, substitute ground red pepper

Place egg yolks, salt, pepper and cream in blender and blend for a few seconds on HIGH until smooth and frothy. Remove center of blender lid. Turn blender to HIGH and pour in half melted hot butter in a thin, steady stream. Add lemon juice and stream in remaining butter. Keep warm in double boiler. Do not overheat.

chunky ranch potatoes

SERVINGS: 8 | PREP TIME: 10 MINUTES
HIGH: 4 TO 6 HOURS | LOW: 7 TO 9 HOURS

3   pounds medium red potatoes,
    unpeeled and quartered

1   cup water

½   cup prepared ranch dressing

½   cup grated Parmesan or
    Cheddar cheese (optional)

¼   cup minced chives

Place potatoes in 4½-quart **CROCK-POT**® slow cooker. Add water. Cover; cook on LOW 7 to 9 hours or on HIGH 4 to 6 hours or until potatoes are tender.

Stir in ranch dressing, cheese, if desired, and chives. Use spoon to break up potatoes into chunks. Serve hot or cold.

bacon & cheese brunch potatoes

SERVINGS: 6 | PREP TIME: 10 MINUTES
HIGH: 3½ HOURS | LOW: 6 HOURS

3 medium russet potatoes (about 2 pounds), peeled and cut into 1-inch dice

1 cup chopped onion

½ teaspoon seasoned salt

4 slices crisply cooked bacon, crumbled

1 cup (4 ounces) shredded sharp Cheddar cheese

1 tablespoon water or chicken broth

Coat 4½-quart **CROCK-POT®** slow cooker with nonstick cooking spray. Place half of potatoes in slow cooker. Sprinkle one-half of onion and seasoned salt over potatoes; top with one-half of bacon and cheese. Repeat layers, ending with cheese. Sprinkle water over top.

Cover; cook on LOW 6 hours or on HIGH 3½ hours or until potatoes and onion are tender. Stir gently to mix and serve hot.

breakfast bake

SERVINGS: 6 TO 8 | PREP TIME: 15 MINUTES

HIGH: 2 TO 2½ HOURS | LOW: 3 TO 3½ HOURS

3   to 4 cups diced crusty bread
    (¾- to 1-inch dice)

½   pound bacon, cut into ½-inch
    dice

2   cups sliced mushrooms

2   cups torn fresh spinach

8   eggs

½   cup milk

¾   cup roasted red peppers,
    drained and chopped

1   cup shredded cheese, such as
    Cheddar or Monterey Jack

    Salt and black pepper, to taste

Coat 4½-quart **CROCK-POT®** slow cooker with nonstick cooking spray. Add bread.

Heat skillet on medium heat until hot. Cook bacon until crispy. Remove and discard all but 1 tablespoon of drippings. Add mushrooms and spinach to skillet and toss to coat. Cook 1 to 2 minutes or until spinach wilts. Transfer to **CROCK-POT®** slow cooker; toss to combine with bread.

Beat eggs and milk in medium bowl. Stir in red peppers, cheese, salt and black pepper. Pour into **CROCK-POT®** slow cooker.

Cover; cook on LOW 3 to 3½ hours or on HIGH 2 to 2½ hours or until eggs are firm but still moist. Adjust seasonings, if desired.

cheese grits with chiles & bacon

SERVINGS: 4 | PREP TIME: 15 MINUTES
LOW: 4 HOURS

6   slices bacon, divided

1   serrano or jalapeño pepper,
    cored, seeded and minced*

1   large shallot or small onion,
    finely chopped

1   cup grits**

4   cups chicken broth

¼   teaspoon black pepper

    Salt, to taste

½   cup half-and-half

1   cup shredded Cheddar cheese

2   tablespoons finely chopped
    green onion, green part
    only

*Hot peppers can sting and irritate the skin, so wear rubber gloves when handling peppers and do not touch eyes.

**You may use coarse, instant, yellow or stone-ground grits.

Fry bacon on both sides in medium skillet until crisp. Remove bacon and drain on paper towels. Cut 2 strips into bite-size pieces. Refrigerate and reserve remaining bacon. Place cut-up bacon in 5-quart **CROCK-POT®** slow cooker.

Drain all but 1 tablespoon bacon drippings from skillet. Add pepper and shallot. Cook and stir over medium-high heat 1 minute or until shallot is transparent and lightly browned. Transfer to 4½-quart **CROCK-POT®** slow cooker. Stir in grits, broth, pepper and salt. Cover; cook on LOW 4 hours.

Stir in half-and-half and cheese. Sprinkle on green onion. Chop remaining bacon into bite-size pieces and stir into grits or sprinkle on top of each serving. Serve immediately.

chocolate-stuffed
slow cooker french toast

SERVINGS: 6 | PREP TIME: 15 MINUTES
HIGH: 3 HOURS | LOW: 6 HOURS

6   slices (¾ inch thick) day-old challah*

½   cup semisweet chocolate chips, divided

6   eggs

3   cups half-and-half

⅔   cup sugar

1   teaspoon vanilla

¼   teaspoon salt

     Powdered sugar or warm maple syrup

     Fresh fruit (optional)

Challah is usually braided. If you use brioche or another rich egg bread, slice bread to fit baking dish.

Generously butter 2½-quart baking dish that fits inside 6-quart **CROCK-POT®** slow cooker. Arrange 2 bread slices in bottom of dish. Sprinkle on ¼ cup chocolate chips. Add 2 more bread slices. Sprinkle with remaining ¼ cup chocolate chips. Top with remaining 2 bread slices.

Beat eggs in large bowl. Stir in half-and-half, sugar, vanilla and salt. Pour egg mixture over bread layers. Press bread into liquid. Set aside 10 minutes or until bread has absorbed liquid. Cover dish with buttered foil, butter side down.

Pour 1 inch hot water into slow cooker. Add baking dish. Cover; cook on LOW 6 hours or on HIGH 3 hours or until toothpick inserted into center comes out clean. Remove dish and let stand 10 minutes to firm up. Serve with powdered sugar. Garnish with fresh fruit, if desired.

ham & cheddar brunch strata

SERVINGS: 6 TO 8 | PREP TIME: 10 MINUTES
LOW: 3½ HOURS

8   ounces French bread, torn into small pieces

2   cups shredded sharp Cheddar cheese, divided

1½   cups diced ham

½   cup finely chopped green onions (white and green parts), divided

4   large eggs

1   cup half-and-half or whole milk

1   tablespoon Worcestershire sauce

⅛   teaspoon ground red pepper

Coat 4½-quart **CROCK-POT®** slow cooker with nonstick cooking spray. Cut parchment paper to fit bottom of stoneware* and press into place. Spray paper lightly with nonstick cooking spray.

Layer in following order: bread, 1½ cups cheese, ham and all but 2 tablespoons green onions.

Whisk eggs, half-and-half, Worcestershire sauce and red pepper in small bowl. Pour evenly over layered ingredients in **CROCK-POT®** slow cooker. Cover; cook on LOW 3½ hours or until knife inserted into center comes out clean. Turn off heat. Sprinkle evenly with reserved ½ cup cheese and 2 tablespoons green onions. Let stand, covered, 10 minutes or until cheese has melted.

To serve, run a knife or rubber spatula around outer edges, lifting bottom slightly. Invert onto plate and peel off paper. Invert again onto serving plate.

To cut parchment paper to fit, trace around the stoneware bottom, then cut the paper slightly smaller to fit. If parchment paper is unavailable, substitute waxed paper.

banana nut bread

SERVINGS: 6 | PREP TIME: 15 MINUTES
HIGH: 2 TO 3 HOURS

½ cup chopped walnuts

⅓ cup butter or margarine

⅔ cup sugar

2 eggs, well beaten

2 tablespoons dark corn syrup

3 ripe bananas, well mashed

1¾ cups all-purpose flour

2 teaspoons baking powder

½ teaspoon salt

¼ teaspoon baking soda

Grease and flour inside of 3-quart **CROCK-POT®** slow cooker.

Cream butter in large bowl with electric mixer until fluffy. Slowly add sugar, eggs, corn syrup and mashed bananas. Beat until smooth.

Sift together flour, baking powder, salt and baking soda in small bowl. Slowly beat flour mixture into creamed mixture. Add walnuts and mix thoroughly. Pour into **CROCK-POT®** slow cooker. Cover; cook on HIGH 2 to 3 hours.

Let cool, then turn bread out onto serving platter.

Note: Banana nut bread has always been a favorite way to use up those overripe bananas. Not only is it delicious, but it also freezes well for future use.

Tip: For a 5-, 6- or 7-quart **CROCK-POT®** slow cooker, you may double all ingredients.

cheesy shrimp on grits

SERVINGS: 6 | PREP TIME: 15 MINUTES
HIGH: 2 HOURS PLUS 20 MINUTES | LOW: 4 HOURS PLUS 20 MINUTES

1	cup finely chopped green bell pepper
1	cup finely chopped red bell pepper
½	cup thinly sliced celery
1	bunch green onions, chopped, divided
¼	cup (½ stick) butter, cubed
1¼	teaspoons seafood seasoning
2	bay leaves
¼	teaspoon ground red pepper
1	pound uncooked shrimp, peeled, deveined and cleaned
5⅓	cups water
1⅓	cups quick-cooking grits
8	ounces shredded sharp Cheddar cheese
¼	cup whipping cream or half-and-half

Coat 4½-quart **CROCK-POT®** slow cooker with nonstick cooking spray. Add bell peppers, celery, all but ½ cup green onions, butter, seafood seasoning, bay leaves and red pepper. Cover; cook on LOW 4 hours or on HIGH 2 hours.

Turn CROCK-POT® slow cooker to HIGH. Add shrimp. Cover; cook 15 minutes longer. Meanwhile, bring water to a boil in medium saucepan. Add grits and cook according to directions on package.

Discard bay leaves from shrimp mixture. Stir in cheese, cream and remaining ½ cup green onions. Cook 5 minutes longer or until cheese has melted. Serve over grits.

Variation: This dish is also delicious served over polenta.

apple-cinnamon breakfast risotto

SERVINGS: 6 | PREP TIME: 10 MINUTES
HIGH: 1½ TO 2 HOURS | LOW: 3 TO 4 HOURS

¼ cup (½ stick) butter

4 medium Granny Smith apples, peeled, cored and diced into ½-inch cubes (about 1½ pounds)

1½ teaspoons ground cinnamon

¼ teaspoon ground allspice

¼ teaspoon salt

1½ cups arborio rice

½ cup packed dark brown sugar

4 cups unfiltered apple juice, at room temperature*

1 teaspoon vanilla

Optional toppings: dried cranberries, sliced almonds, milk

*If unfiltered apple juice is unavailable, use any apple juice.

Coat 4½-quart **CROCK-POT®** slow cooker with nonstick cooking spray; set aside. Melt butter in large skillet over medium-high heat. Add apples, cinnamon, allspice and salt. Cook and stir 3 to 5 minutes or until apples begin to release juices. Transfer to slow cooker.

Add rice and stir to coat. Sprinkle brown sugar evenly over top. Add apple juice and vanilla. Cover; cook on LOW 3 to 4 hours or on HIGH 1½ to 2 hours or until all liquid is absorbed. Ladle risotto into bowls and serve hot. Garnish as desired.

savory sausage bread pudding

SERVINGS: 4 TO 6 | PREP TIME: 10 MINUTES

LOW: 4 TO 5 HOURS

4   eggs

2   cups milk or 1 cup half-and-half and 1 cup milk

¼   teaspoon salt

¼   teaspoon black pepper

¼   teaspoon crushed dried thyme

⅛   teaspoon crushed red pepper flakes

1   package (10 ounces) smoky breakfast sausage links, cut into ½-inch pieces

¾   cup shredded Cheddar cheese

2   cups day-old bread cubes, cut into ½-inch pieces

Beat eggs in large bowl. Add milk, salt, pepper, thyme and pepper flakes; stir in well. Stir in sausage, cheese and bread. Press bread into egg mixture. Set aside 10 minutes or until bread has absorbed liquid.

Generously butter 2-quart baking dish that fits inside 5- or 6-quart **CROCK-POT**® slow cooker. Pour sausage mixture into dish. Cover dish with buttered foil, butter side down.

Pour 1 inch hot water into **CROCK-POT**® slow cooker. Add baking dish. Cover; cook on LOW 4 to 5 hours or until tester inserted into center comes out clean.

french toast bread pudding

SERVINGS: 6 TO 8 | PREP TIME: 15 MINUTES
HIGH: 1½ TO 2 HOURS | LOW: 3 TO 4 HOURS

2	tablespoons packed dark brown sugar
2½	teaspoons ground cinnamon
1	loaf (24 ounces) Texas-toast-style bread*
2	cups whipping cream
2	cups half-and-half
2	teaspoons vanilla
¼	teaspoon salt
4	egg yolks
1¼	cups granulated sugar
¼	teaspoon ground nutmeg
	Maple syrup
	Whipped cream (optional)

*If unavailable, cut day-old 24-ounce loaf of white sandwich bread into 1-inch-thick slices.

Coat 3½-quart **CROCK-POT®** slow cooker with nonstick cooking spray. Combine brown sugar and cinnamon in small bowl. Reserve 1 tablespoon; set aside.

Cut bread slices in half diagonally. Cover bottom of **CROCK-POT®** slow cooker with bread slices arranged in single layer. Sprinkle 1 rounded tablespoon cinnamon mixture evenly over bread. Repeat with remaining bread and cinnamon mixture, keeping layers as flat as possible. Tuck any remaining bread into vertical spaces.

Bring cream, half-and-half, vanilla and salt to boil in large saucepan over medium heat stirring constantly. Reduce heat to low.

Meanwhile, whisk egg yolks and granulated sugar in medium bowl. Continue to whisk quickly while adding ¼ cup of hot cream mixture.** Add warmed egg mixture to saucepan and increase heat to medium-high. Cook and stir about 5 minutes or until mixture thickens slightly. Do not boil.

Remove from heat and stir in nutmeg. Pour mixture over bread and press bread down lightly. Sprinkle reserved cinnamon mixture on top. Cover; cook on LOW 3 to 4 hours or on HIGH 1½ to 2 hours or until toothpick inserted into center comes out clean.

Turn off **CROCK-POT®** slow cooker and uncover. Let stand 10 minutes before spooning into bowls. Serve with maple syrup and whipped cream, if desired.

**Place bowl on damp towel to prevent slipping.

whoa breakfast

SERVINGS: 4 TO 6 | PREP TIME: 10 MINUTES
HIGH: 4 HOURS | LOW: 8 HOURS

1½ cups uncooked steel-cut or
    old-fashioned oats

3   cups water

2   cups chopped peeled apples

¼   cup sliced almonds

½   teaspoon ground cinnamon

Combine all ingredients in 4½-quart **CROCK-POT®** slow cooker. Cover; cook on LOW 8 hours or on HIGH 4 hours.

whole-grain banana bread

SERVINGS: 8 TO 10 | PREP TIME: 30 MINUTES
HIGH: 2 TO 3 HOURS | LOW: 4 TO 6 HOURS

¼ cup plus 2 tablespoons wheat germ, divided

⅔ cup butter, softened

1 cup sugar

2 eggs

1 cup mashed bananas (2 to 3 bananas)

1 teaspoon vanilla

1 cup all-purpose flour

1 cup whole wheat pastry flour

1 teaspoon baking soda

½ teaspoon salt

½ cup chopped walnuts or pecans (optional)

Spray 1-quart casserole, soufflé dish or other high-sided baking pan with nonstick cooking spray. Sprinkle dish with 2 tablespoons wheat germ.

Beat butter and sugar in large bowl with electric mixer until fluffy. Add eggs one at a time; beat until blended. Add bananas and vanilla; beat until smooth.

Gradually stir in flours, remaining ¼ cup wheat germ, baking soda and salt. Stir in nuts, if desired. Pour batter into prepared dish; place in 4½-quart **CROCK-POT®** slow cooker. Cover; cook on LOW 4 to 6 hours or on HIGH 2 to 3 hours or until edges begin to brown and toothpick inserted into center comes out clean.

Remove dish from **CROCK-POT®** slow cooker. Cool on wire rack about 10 minutes. Remove bread from dish; cool completely on wire rack.

Everyday Gourmet

ham & sage-stuffed cornish hens

SERVINGS: 4 | PREP TIME: 45 MINUTES
HIGH: 3 TO 4 HOURS | LOW: 5 TO 6 HOURS

1   **cup plus 3 tablespoons sliced celery, divided**

1   **cup sliced leek (white part only)**

2   **tablespoons butter, divided**

¼   **cup finely diced onion**

¼   **cup diced prosciutto or smoked ham**

1   **cup seasoned dry stuffing mix**

1   **cup chicken broth**

1   **tablespoon finely chopped fresh sage leaves or 1 teaspoon ground sage**

4   **Cornish game hens (about 1½ pounds each)**

     Salt and black pepper

Coat 5- to 6-quart **CROCK-POT®** slow cooker with nonstick cooking spray. Toss 1 cup celery and 1 cup leek in **CROCK-POT®** slow cooker.

Melt 1 tablespoon butter in large nonstick skillet over medium heat. Add remaining 3 tablespoons celery, onion and prosciutto. Cook, stirring frequently, 5 minutes or until onion is soft. Stir in stuffing mix, chicken broth and sage. Transfer mixture to medium bowl and set aside to cool slightly. Save skillet for further use.

Rinse hens and pat dry; sprinkle inside and out with salt and pepper. Gently spoon stuffing into birds' cavities. Tie each hen's drumsticks together with kitchen twine.

Melt remaining tablespoon butter in same skillet over medium-high heat. Place 2 hens, breast sides down, in skillet and cook until skins brown, turning to brown all sides. Transfer to prepared **CROCK-POT®** slow cooker. Repeat with remaining hens. Cover and cook on LOW 5 to 6 hours on HIGH 3 to 4 hours. To serve, remove twine and place hens on serving platter with vegetables; spoon cooking broth over hens.

middle-eastern spiced beef, tomatoes & beans

SERVINGS: ABOUT 4 | PREP TIME: 30 MINUTES
HIGH: 4 HOURS | LOW: 8 HOURS

2 tablespoons extra-virgin olive oil, divided

1½ pounds lean boneless beef chuck roast, cut into 1-inch pieces, divided

1 can (14½ ounces) diced tomatoes with peppers and onions, undrained

6 ounces fresh green beans, trimmed and broken into 1-inch pieces

1 cup chopped onion

½ teaspoon ground cinnamon

¼ teaspoon ground allspice

1½ teaspoons sugar

¼ teaspoon garlic powder

½ teaspoon salt or to taste

¼ teaspoon black pepper

Cooked rice or couscous (optional)

Heat 2 teaspoons oil in large skillet over medium-high heat. Add half of beef cubes and cook, stirring frequently, until browned on all sides. Transfer to 3½- to 4-quart **CROCK-POT®** slow cooker. Add additional 2 teaspoons oil and repeat with remaining beef.

Stir in tomatoes, beans, onion, cinnamon, allspice, sugar and garlic powder. Cover and cook on LOW 8 hours or on HIGH 4 hours.

Stir in salt, pepper and remaining 2 teaspoons oil and let stand uncovered 15 minutes to allow flavors to absorb and thicken slightly. Serve as is or over cooked rice or couscous, if desired.

pork & anaheim stew

SERVINGS: 4 TO 6 | PREP TIME: 30 MINUTES
HIGH: 5 HOURS | LOW: 10 HOURS

2   tablespoons extra-virgin olive oil, divided

1½   pounds boneless pork shoulder, trimmed of fat and cut into ½-inch pieces

6   Anaheim peppers, split in half lengthwise, seeded and sliced*

4   cloves garlic, minced

1   pound tomatillos, papery skins removed, rinsed and chopped

2   cups chopped onion

1   can (15½ ounces) yellow hominy, rinsed and drained

1   can (14½ ounces) 99% fat free chicken broth

2   teaspoons chili powder

1   teaspoon ground cumin

1   teaspoon dried oregano leaves

1½   teaspoons sugar

1   teaspoon liquid smoke

½   teaspoon salt, or to taste

*Anaheim peppers can sting and irritate the skin, so wear rubber gloves when handling peppers and do not touch your eyes.

Heat 1 teaspoon oil in large skillet over medium-high heat. Add half of pork to skillet and cook, stirring frequently, until browned on all sides. Transfer to 4½-quart **CROCK-POT®** slow cooker. Add another teaspoon oil to same skillet and repeat with remaining pork.

Add another 1 teaspoon oil to same skillet and add Anaheim chiles. Cook 5 minutes, stirring frequently, or until very brown along edges. Using 2 utensils to toss chiles while cooking. (Turn ventilation system to maximum setting before adding chiles to skillet.) Add garlic to chiles and cook another 15 seconds, stirring constantly. Pour over pork.

Stir in tomatillos, onion, hominy, broth, chili powder, cumin, oregano and sugar. Cover and cook on LOW 10 hours or on HIGH 5 hours.

Stir in remaining 1 tablespoon oil, liquid smoke and salt. Serve immediately or cover and refrigerate overnight (flavors intensify with time).

merlot beef chili with horseradish sour cream

SERVINGS: 4 | PREP TIME: 30 MINUTES
HIGH: 6 HOURS | LOW: 12 HOURS

2	tablespoons olive oil, divided
1	pound boneless beef chuck roast, cut into ½-inch pieces
1	can (10½ ounces) condensed beef broth
¼	cup Merlot or dry red wine
1	can (14½ ounces) stewed tomatoes with Italian seasonings, undrained
1	can (8 ounces) tomato sauce
½	cup chopped green bell pepper
½	cup chopped onion
2	cloves garlic, minced
2	teaspoons sugar
¾	teaspoon instant coffee granules
2	bay leaves
1	tablespoon chili powder
½	teaspoon coarsely ground black pepper
¾	cup sour cream
3	tablespoons prepared horseradish
1	teaspoon salt, or more to taste, divided
	Cooked egg noodles (optional)

Heat 1 tablespoon olive oil in large skillet over high heat. Add beef and cook, stirring frequently, until browned on all sides. Transfer to 3½- to 4-quart **CROCK-POT®** slow cooker. Stir in broth, wine, stewed tomatoes and their juice, tomato sauce, bell pepper, onion, garlic, sugar, coffee granules, bay leaves, chili powder and pepper. Cover and cook on LOW 12 hours or on HIGH 6 hours or until beef is very tender.

Meanwhile, combine sour cream, horseradish and salt to taste in small bowl. Refrigerate in airtight container until needed.

Stir to break up large pieces of beef with potato masher or wooden spoon. Stir in remaining 1 tablespoon oil and salt and pepper to taste. Serve as is or over cooked egg noodles; top with horseradish sour cream just before serving.

duck confit & mushroom salad

SERVINGS: 4 | PREP TIME: 35 MINUTES
HIGH: 4 TO 5 HOURS | LOW: 6½ TO 7½ HOURS

½ pound bacon, fat trimmed, diced

2 shallots, thinly sliced

8 ounces fresh mushrooms such as shiitake, oyster, chanterelles or a combination

1 tablespoon Dijon mustard

1 tablespoon sherry wine vinegar

3 tablespoons extra-virgin olive oil

Kosher salt and pepper

Sugar

1½ pounds frisée lettuce or mesclun lettuce mix

2 cups Duck Confit (recipe follows)

DUCK CONFIT

1 tablespoon black peppercorns

1 teaspoon coriander seeds

½ teaspoon nutmeg, freshly grated

1 clove

1 teaspoon dried thyme

1 bay leaf

½ teaspoon ground ginger

1 teaspoon Kosher salt, divided

1 whole duck (3 to 4 pounds)

Cook bacon in large skillet over medium-low heat to desired doneness. Transfer bacon to paper towel-lined plate to drain and return pan to heat.

Add shallots to pan and cook for two minutes, stirring often. Add mushrooms, season lightly with salt and pepper and cook until tender. Remove from heat.

Whisk together Dijon mustard and vinegar in a medium bowl. Whisking constantly, slowly pour in thin stream of oil until dressing thickens. Season to taste with salt, pepper and sugar.

Combine frisee, mushrooms, bacon and 2 cups Duck Confit in large bowl. Pour dressing over and toss to coat. Serve immediately.

DUCK CONFIT

Preheat broiler. Place all ingredients except salt in a coffee grinder and grind for 15 seconds.

Sprinkle 1½ teaspoons salt and half of spice mixture over breast side of duck. Place breast-side down in broiler safe dish. with sides at least 1½ inches high. Season back of duck with remaining salt spice mix.

Place duck in broiler and cook about 10 minutes until spices are fragrant and skin is starting to brown. Roll duck onto its side and broil 10 minutes more to brown side; repeat with last 2 sides of duck, rendering fat and browning all sides (about 40 minutes total).

Transfer duck to 5- or 6-quart **CROCK-POT®** slow cooker. Cover and cook on LOW 6 to 7 hours or on HIGH 3½ hours or until duck is cooked through and tender.

Cool in **CROCK-POT®** slow cooker about 1 hour. Remove duck, reserving drippings for other use. Skin and debone duck. Refrigerate until needed.

italian braised short ribs in red wine

SERVINGS: 4 TO 6 | PREP TIME: 20 MINUTES
HIGH: 6 TO 8 HOURS | LOW: 10 TO 12 HOURS

3 pounds beef short ribs, trimmed of excess fat

Salt and black pepper

1 tablespoon vegetable oil, plus more if needed

2 large onions, sliced

2 cloves garlic, minced

2 packages (8 ounces each) baby bella or cremini mushrooms, cleaned and quartered

2 cups red wine

2 cups beef broth

2 teaspoons Italian seasoning

Salt and black pepper

Mashed potatoes or polenta

Coat 5½-quart **CROCK-POT®** slow cooker with nonstick cooking spray. Season short ribs with salt and pepper. Heat oil in large skillet over medium-high heat. Brown ribs on all sides, working in batches and adding additional oil as needed. Transfer to prepared **CROCK-POT®** slow cooker as batches are finished.

Return skillet to heat. Add onions and cook, stirring frequently, until translucent (3 to 5 minutes). Stir in remaining ingredients except potatoes and bring mixture to simmer. Cook 3 minutes then pour over short ribs. Cover and cook on LOW 10 to 12 hours or on HIGH 6 to 8 hours or until beef is tender. Season to taste with salt and pepper. Transfer ribs and mushrooms to serving plate. Strain cooking liquid; serve with mashed potatoes or polenta and sauce with cooking liquid.

sauvignon blanc beef with beets & thyme

SERVINGS: 6 | PREP TIME: 30 MINUTES

HIGH: 4 TO 5 HOURS | LOW: 8 TO 10 HOURS

1   pound red or yellow beets, scrubbed and quartered

2   tablespoons extra-virgin olive oil

1   beef chuck roast (about 3 pounds)

1   medium yellow onion, peeled and quartered

2   cloves garlic, minced

5   sprigs fresh thyme

1   bay leaf

2   whole cloves

1   cup chicken broth

1   cup Sauvignon Blanc or other white wine

2   tablespoons tomato paste

     Salt and black pepper, to taste

Layer beets evenly in 4½-quart **CROCK-POT®** slow cooker.

Heat oil in large skillet over medium heat. Sear roast on all sides 4 to 5 minutes, turning as it browns. Add onion and garlic after turning roast to sear its last side. Transfer all ingredients to **CROCK-POT®** slow cooker.

Add thyme, bay leaf and cloves. Combine broth, wine and tomato paste in medium bowl. Add salt and pepper. Mix well to combine. Pour over roast and beets. Cover; cook on LOW 8 to 10 hours or on HIGH 4 to 5 hours or or until roast and beets are tender.

basil chicken merlot with wild mushrooms

SERVINGS: 4 TO 6 | PREP TIME: 45 MINUTES
HIGH: 3 TO 4 HOURS | LOW: 7 TO 9 HOURS

3 tablespoons extra-virgin olive oil, divided

1 roasting chicken, skinned and cut into individual pieces (about 3 pounds)

1½ cups cremini mushrooms, thickly sliced

1 medium yellow onion, diced

2 cloves garlic, minced

1 cup chicken broth

1 can (6 ounces) tomato paste

⅓ cup Merlot or other dry red wine

2 teaspoons sugar

1 teaspoon ground oregano

¼ teaspoon salt

¼ teaspoon black pepper

2 tablespoons minced fresh basil

3 cups cooked ziti pasta, drained

Grated Romano cheese (optional)

Heat 1½ to 2 tablespoons oil in skillet over medium heat until hot. Brown half of chicken pieces on each side 3 to 5 minutes, turning once. Remove with slotted spoon and repeat with remaining chicken. Set chicken aside.

Heat remaining oil in skillet and add mushrooms, onion and garlic. Cook and stir 7 to 8 minutes or until onions are soft. Transfer to 4½-quart **CROCK-POT®** slow cooker. Top with reserved chicken.

Combine broth, tomato paste, wine, sugar, oregano, salt and pepper in medium bowl. Pour sauce over chicken. Cover; cook on LOW 7 to 9 hours or on HIGH 3 to 4 hours.

Stir in basil. Place pasta in large serving bowl or on platter. Ladle chicken and mushrooms over pasta and spoon extra sauce over all. Garnish with Romano cheese.

autumn herbed chicken with fennel & squash

SERVINGS: 6 | PREP TIME: 30 MINUTES
HIGH: 2½ TO 4½ HOURS | LOW: 5 TO 7 HOURS

3 to 4 pounds chicken thighs

Salt and black pepper, to taste

All-purpose flour, as needed

2 tablespoons olive oil

1 fennel bulb, thinly sliced

½ butternut squash, peeled, seeded and cut into ¾-inch cubes

1 teaspoon dried thyme

¾ cup walnuts (optional)

¾ cup chicken broth

½ cup apple cider or juice

Cooked rice or pasta

¼ cup fresh basil, sliced into ribbons

2 teaspoons fresh rosemary, finely minced

Season chicken on all sides with salt and pepper, then lightly coat with flour. Heat oil in skillet over medium heat until hot. Brown chicken in batches to prevent crowding. Brown on each side 3 to 5 minutes, turning once. Remove with slotted spoon. Transfer to 4½-quart **CROCK-POT®** slow cooker.

Add fennel, squash and thyme. Stir well to combine. Add walnuts, if desired, broth and cider. Cover and cook on LOW 5 to 7 hours or on HIGH 2½ to 4½ hours.

Serve over rice or pasta and garnish with basil and rosemary.

braised sea bass with aromatic vegetables

SERVINGS: 6 | PREP TIME: 15 MINUTES
HIGH: 3 TO 4 HOURS | LOW: 6 TO 8 HOURS

2 tablespoons butter or olive oil

2 bulbs fennel, thinly sliced

3 large carrots, julienned

3 large leeks, cleaned and thinly sliced

   Kosher salt and pepper

6 fillets sea bass or other firm-fleshed white fish (2 to 3 pounds total)

Melt butter in large skillet over medium-high heat. Add fennel, carrots and leeks. Cook and stir until beginning to soften and lightly brown. Season with salt and pepper.

Arrange half of vegetables in bottom of 4½-quart **CROCK-POT®** slow cooker.

Season fish with salt and pepper and place on vegetables in **CROCK-POT®** slow cooker. Top with remaining vegetables.

Cover and cook on LOW 2 to 3 hours or on HIGH for 1 to 1½ hours or until fish is cooked through.

turkey piccata

SERVINGS: 4 | PREP TIME: 15 MINUTES
LOW: 2 HOURS

2½ tablespoons all-purpose flour

¼ teaspoon salt, or to taste

¼ teaspoon black pepper

1 pound turkey breast meat, cut into short strips

1 tablespoon butter

1 tablespoon olive oil

½ cup chicken broth

2 teaspoons freshly squeezed lemon juice

Grated peel of 1 lemon

2 tablespoons finely chopped fresh parsley

2 cups cooked rice (optional)

Combine flour, salt and pepper in food storage bag. Add turkey strips and shake well to coat. Heat butter and oil in large skillet over medium-high heat until hot. Add turkey strips in single layer. Brown on all sides, about 2 minutes per side. Transfer to 5-quart **CROCK-POT®** slow cooker, arranging on bottom in single layer.

Pour broth into skillet. Cook and stir to scrape up any browned bits. Pour into **CROCK-POT®** slow cooker. Add lemon juice and peel. Cover; cook on LOW 2 hours. Sprinkle with parsley before serving. Serve over rice, if desired.

slow cooker cassoulet

SERVINGS: 4 | PREP TIME: 30 MINUTES
HIGH: 4 HOURS | LOW: 8 HOURS

1 **pound dried white beans, such as Great Northern**

Boiling water

1 **tablespoon butter**

1 **tablespoon canola oil**

4 **veal shanks, 1½ inches thick, tied for cooking**

3 **cups beef broth**

4 **ounces maple-smoked bacon or pancetta, diced**

3 **cloves garlic, smashed**

1 **sprig fresh thyme**

1 **sprig fresh savory**

2 **whole cloves**

Salt and pepper, to taste

4 **mild Italian sausages, fully cooked**

Rinse and sort beans and place in large bowl; cover completely with water. Soak 6 to 8 hours or overnight. (To quick-soak beans, place beans in large saucepan; cover with water. Bring to a boil over high heat. Boil 2 minutes. Remove from heat. Cover and soak 1 hour.) Drain beans; discard water.

Heat butter and oil in large skillet over medium-high heat. Sear shanks on all sides until browned. Transfer to 4½-quart **CROCK-POT®** slow cooker. Add broth, bacon, garlic, beans, herbs and cloves. Add enough water to cover beans, if needed. Cover and cook on LOW 8 hours or on HIGH 4 hours. Check liquid halfway through cooking time and add boiling water as needed to cover beans.

Before serving, season with salt and pepper. Slice sausages; serve with cassoulet.

beef roast with dark rum sauce

SERVINGS: 6 | PREP TIME: 30 MINUTES
LOW: 5 TO 7 HOURS

1	teaspoon ground allspice
½	teaspoon salt
½	teaspoon black pepper
¼	teaspoon ground cloves
1	beef rump roast (about 3 pounds)
2	tablespoons extra-virgin olive oil
1	cup dark rum, divided
½	cup beef broth
2	cloves garlic, minced
2	bay leaves, broken in half
½	cup packed dark brown sugar
¼	cup lime juice

Combine allspice, salt, pepper and cloves in small bowl. Rub spices onto all sides of roast.

Heat oil in skillet over medium heat until hot. Sear beef on all sides, turning as it browns. Transfer to 4½-quart **CROCK-POT®** slow cooker. Add ½ cup rum, broth, garlic and bay leaves. Cover; cook on LOW 1 hour.

Combine combine remaining rum, brown sugar and lime juice in small bowl. Stir well. Pour over roast. Continue cooking on LOW 4 to 6 hours or until beef is fork-tender. Baste beef occasionally with sauce.

Remove and slice roast. Spoon sauce over beef to serve.

weeknight chili

SERVINGS: 4 | PREP TIME: 15 MINUTES
HIGH: 2 TO 3 HOURS | LOW: 4 TO 6 HOURS

1   pound ground beef or ground turkey

1   package (1¼ ounces) chili seasoning mix

1   can (about 14 ounces) diced tomatoes with green chiles, undrained

1   can (about 15 ounces) red kidney beans, rinsed and drained

1   can (8 ounces) tomato sauce

1   cup shredded Cheddar cheese

Brown ground beef in large skillet, stirring to break up meat; drain fat. Stir in seasoning mix.

Place beef, tomatoes, beans and tomato sauce in 4½-quart **CROCK-POT®** slow cooker. Cover and cook on LOW 4 to 6 hours or on HIGH 2 to 3 hours. Top each serving with cheese.

maple whiskey glazed beef brisket

SERVINGS: 4 TO 6 | PREP TIME: 20 MINUTES
HIGH: 3½ TO 4½ HOURS | LOW: 7 TO 9 HOURS

1 teaspoon ground red pepper

1 tablespoon coarse salt

½ teaspoon freshly ground black pepper

1½ to 2 pounds beef brisket, scored with a knife on both sides

2 tablespoons olive oil

½ cup maple syrup

¼ cup whiskey

2 tablespoons packed brown sugar

1 tablespoon tomato paste

Juice of 1 orange

2 cloves garlic, mashed

4 thin slices peeled fresh ginger

4 slices orange peel

Combine red pepper, salt and black pepper in small mixing bowl. Rub over brisket. Place brisket in food storage bag. Set aside.

Combine oil, syrup, whiskey, sugar, tomato paste, orange juice, garlic, ginger and orange peel in mixing bowl. Stir to mix. Pour mixture over brisket in food storage bag.

Marinate brisket in refrigerator at least 2 hours or overnight.

Transfer brisket and marinade to 4-quart **CROCK-POT®** slow cooker. Cover; cook on LOW 7 to 9 hours or on HIGH 3½ to 4½ hours, turning brisket once or twice. Adjust seasonings to taste. Slice beef thinly across the grain and serve.

turkey with chunky cherry relish

SERVINGS: 4 TO 6 | PREP TIME: 20 MINUTES
HIGH: 3½ TO 4 HOURS | LOW: 7 TO 8 HOURS

1   bag (16 ounces) frozen dark cherries, coarsely chopped

1   can (about 14 ounces) diced tomatoes with jalapeños

1   package (6 ounces) dried cherry-flavored cranberries or dried cherries, coarsely chopped

2   small onions, thinly sliced

1   small green bell pepper, chopped

½   cup packed brown sugar

2   tablespoons tapioca

1½ tablespoons salt

½   teaspoon ground cinnamon

½   teaspoon black pepper

1   bone-in turkey breast (about 2½ to 3 pounds)

1   tablespoon cornstarch

2   tablespoons water

Place cherries, tomatoes, cranberries, onions, bell pepper, brown sugar, tapioca, salt, cinnamon and black pepper in 6- to 7-quart **CROCK-POT®** slow cooker; mix well.

Place turkey on top of mixture. Cover; cook on LOW 7 to 8 hours or on HIGH 3½ to 4 hours or until temperature registers 170°F on meat thermometer inserted into thickest part of breast, not touching bone. Remove turkey from **CROCK-POT®** slow cooker; keep warm.

Turn CROCK-POT® slow cooker to HIGH. Stir cornstarch into water in small bowl, making smooth paste. Stir into cherry mixture. Cook, uncovered, on HIGH 15 minutes or until sauce is thickened. Adjust seasonings, if desired. Slice turkey and top with relish.

chipotle chicken casserole

SERVINGS: 6 | PREP TIME: 15 MINUTES
HIGH: 3½ TO 4 HOURS | LOW: 7 TO 8 HOURS

1	pound boneless skinless chicken thighs, cut into cubes
1	teaspoon salt
1	teaspoon ground cumin
1	bay leaf
1	chipotle pepper in adobo sauce, minced
1	medium onion, diced
1	can (15 ounces) navy beans, rinsed and drained
1	can (15 ounces) black beans, rinsed and drained
1	can (14½ ounces) crushed tomatoes, undrained
1½	cups chicken broth
½	cup orange juice
¼	cup chopped fresh cilantro (optional)

Combine chicken, salt, cumin, bay leaf, chipotle pepper, onion, beans, tomatoes with juice, broth and orange juice in 3½-quart **CROCK-POT®** slow cooker. Cover; cook on LOW 7 to 8 hours or on HIGH 3½ to 4 hours. Remove bay leaf before serving. Garnish with cilantro.

scallops in fresh tomato & herb sauce

SERVINGS: 4 | PREP TIME: 15 MINUTES
HIGH: 3 TO 4 HOURS | LOW: 6 TO 8 HOURS

2	tablespoons vegetable oil
1	medium red onion, peeled and diced
1	clove garlic, minced
3½	cups fresh tomatoes, peeled*
1	can (12 ounces) tomato pureé
1	can (6 ounces) tomato paste
¼	cup dry red wine
2	tablespoons chopped flat-leaf parsley
1	tablespoon chopped fresh oregano
¼	teaspoon black pepper
1½	pounds fresh scallops, cleaned and drained
	Cooked pasta or rice

To peel tomatoes, place one at a time in simmering water about 10 seconds. (Add 30 seconds if tomatoes are not fully ripened.) Immediately plunge into a bowl of cold water for another 10 seconds. Peel skin with a knife.

Heat oil in skillet over medium heat until hot. Add onion and garlic. Cook and stir 7 to 8 minutes or until onions are soft and translucent. Transfer to 4½-quart **CROCK-POT®** slow cooker.

Add tomatoes, tomato purée, tomato paste, wine, parsley, oregano and pepper. Cover; cook on LOW 6 to 8 hours on HIGH 3 to 4 hours.

Turn CROCK-POT® slow cooker to HIGH. Add scallops. Cook 15 minutes longer or until scallops are just cooked through. Serve over pasta or rice.

sirloin tips with caramelized onion brandy sauce

SERVINGS: 4 | PREP TIME: 10 MINUTES
HIGH: 3 TO 4 HOURS | LOW: 6 TO 8 HOURS

3	tablespoons all-purpose flour
½	teaspoon salt
½	teaspoon crushed black peppercorns
1½	pounds beef sirloin tips, cut into 2-inch pieces
½	cup beef broth
3	tablespoons brandy
1	teaspoon Worcestershire sauce
1	clove garlic, minced
2	tablespoons butter, melted
1	tablespoon packed brown sugar
¼	teaspoon ground red pepper
1	medium sweet onion, thinly sliced and separated into rings
¼	cup heavy cream
	Cooked wild rice or mashed potatoes (optional)
½	cup crumbled Gorgonzola cheese
2	tablespoons finely chopped flat-leaf parsley

Combine flour, salt and peppercorns in large food storage bag. Add beef and shake to coat. Transfer to 4½-quart **CROCK-POT®** slow cooker.

Combine broth, brandy, Worcestershire sauce and garlic in small bowl. Pour over beef.

Combine butter, brown sugar and red pepper in small bowl. Add onion and toss to coat. Transfer to **CROCK-POT®** slow cooker. Cover; cook on LOW 6 to 8 hours or on HIGH 3 to 4 hours.

Turn CROCK-POT® slow cooker to HIGH. Stir in heavy cream. Cover; cook 15 minutes longer.

Serve beef and sauce over wild rice, if desired, and garnish with cheese and parsley.

Elegant Entertaining

chicken croustade

SERVINGS: 6 TO 8 | PREP TIME: 45 MINUTES
LOW: 3 HOURS 20 MINUTES

2 tablespoons canola oil

1½ pounds boneless, skinless chicken breast meat, cut into ¼-inch pieces

Salt and black pepper

1 large portobello mushroom cap

1 shallot, minced

¼ cup white wine

1 tablespoon chopped fresh thyme

¼ teaspoon sweet paprika

¼ teaspoon ground cumin

¼ cup chicken broth

1 package puff pastry shells

1 egg yolk

2 tablespoons cream

3 tablespoons freshly grated Parmesan cheese

Minced and whole chives (optional)

Heat oil in large skillet over medium-high heat. Season chicken with salt and pepper and add to skillet with oil. Allow chicken to brown, untouched, about 4 minutes. Turn gently and brown other side.

Meanwhile, scrape gills from mushroom cap with spoon and discard. Chop mushroom cap into ¼-inch pieces.

Transfer chicken to 4½-quart **CROCK-POT®** slow cooker. Return skillet to heat and add shallot. Cook until shallot softens, 1 to 2 minutes. Stir in white wine, scraping up any brown bits with wooden spoon. Continue to cook until white wine is reduced to about 2 tablespoons, then pour over chicken. Stir mushroom, thyme, paprika, cumin and broth. Add pinch of salt and black pepper. Cover and cook on LOW 3 hours.

Two hours after starting to cook chicken, cook puff pastry shells according to package directions and cool completely.

Twenty minutes before end of cooking time, beat egg yolk and cream together. Stir 1 tablespoon hot cooking liquid into egg mixture. Beat until well combined, then stir into remaining cooking liquid. Continue cooking on LOW, uncovered, 20 minutes. Stir in Parmesan cheese and turn off **CROCK-POT®** slow cooker. Divide chicken filling among puff pastry shells. Serve garnished with chopped chives.

thai coconut chicken meatballs

SERVINGS: 4 TO 5 | PREP TIME: 30 MINUTES

HIGH: 4 TO 4½ HOURS

1	pound ground chicken
2	green onions (white and green parts), chopped
1	clove garlic, minced
2	teaspoons toasted sesame oil
1	teaspoon fish sauce
2	teaspoons mirin
1	tablespoon canola oil
½	cup unsweetened canned coconut milk
¼	cup chicken broth
1	teaspoon Thai red curry paste
2	teaspoons brown sugar
2	teaspoons lime juice
1	tablespoon cornstarch
2	tablespoons cold water

Combine chicken, green onions, garlic, sesame oil, fish sauce and mirin in large bowl. Mix well to combine and shape into meatballs about 1½ inches in diameter.

Heat canola oil in large skillet over medium-high heat. Add meatballs and cook, rolling to brown on all sides. Transfer to 4½-quart **CROCK-POT®** slow cooker. Add coconut milk, chicken broth, curry paste and sugar. Cover and cook on HIGH 3½ to 4 hours. Stir in lime juice.

Stir cornstarch into cold water, mixing until smooth. Stir in additional water as needed to reach consistency of heavy cream. Stir into sauce in **CROCK-POT®** slow cooker. Cook uncovered 10 to 15 minutes until sauce is slightly thickened and evenly coats meatballs.

TIP: Meatballs that are of equal sizes will cook at the same rate and be done at the same time. To ensure your meatballs are the same size, pat seasoned ground meat into an even rectangle and then slice into even rows and columns. Roll each portion into smooth ball.

chicken & asiago stuffed mushrooms

SERVINGS: 4 TO 5 | PREP TIME: 40 MINUTES
HIGH: 2 HOURS | LOW: 4 HOURS

20	large white mushrooms, stems removed and reserved
3	tablespoons extra virgin olive oil, divided
¼	cup finely chopped onion
2	cloves garlic, minced
¼	cup Madeira
½	pound uncooked chicken sausage, removed from casings or ground chicken
1	cup grated Asiago cheese
¼	cup seasoned Italian bread crumbs
3	tablespoons chopped fresh parsley
½	teaspoon salt
¼	teaspoon black pepper

Lightly brush mushroom caps with 1 tablespoon oil and set aside. Finely chop mushroom stems.

Heat remaining 2 tablespoons oil in large nonstick skillet over medium-high heat. Add onion and cook until just beginning to soften, about 1 minute. Add mushroom stems and cook until beginning to brown, 5 to 6 minutes. Stir in garlic and continue cooking 1 minute.

Pour in Madeira and cook until it evaporates, about 1 minute. Add sausage and cook, stirring to break into small pieces, until no longer pink, 3 to 4 minutes. Remove from heat and cool 5 minutes. Stir in cheese, bread crumbs, parsley, salt and pepper.

Divide mushroom-sausage mixture among mushroom caps, pressing slightly to compress. Place stuffed mushroom caps in single layer in 5- to 6½-quart **CROCK-POT®** slow cooker; cover and cook on LOW 4 hours or on HIGH 2 hours or until mushrooms are tender and filling is cooked through.

TIP: Stuffed mushrooms are a great way to impress guests with your home-gourmet cooking skills. These appetizers appear fancy and time-intensive, but they are actually simple with the help of a **CROCK-POT®** slow cooker.

warm moroccan-style bean dip

SERVINGS: 4 TO 6 | PREP TIME: 15 MINUTES
LOW: 6 HOURS

2 teaspoons canola oil

1 small onion, chopped

2 cloves garlic, minced

2 cans (15 ounces each) cannellini beans, rinsed and drained and rinsed

¾ cup canned diced tomatoes, drained

½ teaspoon ground turmeric (optional)

¼ teaspoon ground cinnamon

¼ teaspoon paprika

¼ teaspoon black pepper

¼ teaspoon salt

¼ teaspoon ground cumin

⅛ teaspoon ground cloves

⅛ teaspoon ground red pepper

2 tablespoons plain yogurt

1 tablespoon cool water

¼ teaspoon dried mint (optional)

Warm pita bread, cut into wedges

Heat oil in small skillet over medium-high heat. Add onion and cook until translucent (5 to 6 minutes). Add garlic and cook 45 seconds more. Transfer to 4½-quart **CROCK-POT®** slow cooker. Stir in beans, tomatoes and spices. Cover and cook on LOW 6 hours.

Transfer bean mixture and cooking liquid to food processor or blender and pulse to make coarse paste. Alternatively, use immersion blender to chop beans to coarse paste in **CROCK-POT®** slow cooker. Transfer to serving plate or bowl.

Beat yogurt and cold water together until well combined. Drizzle over bean dip and garnish with dried mint, if desired. Serve warm with pita bread wedges for dipping.

TIP: Moroccan cuisine has a wide array of dishes beyond the most famous couscous. The cuisine makes use of a wide variety of spices; this reflects the many ethnicities that have influenced the country over the centuries. This spice-filled dip is sure to stimulate guests' taste buds and conversation with its combination of exotic flavors.

asian lettuce wraps

SERVINGS: 5 TO 6 | PREP TIME: 15 MINUTES
HIGH: 2 TO 2½ HOURS | LOW: 4 TO 5 HOURS

2 teaspoons canola oil

1½ pounds chicken breast or pork butt, chopped into ¼-inch pieces

2 leeks, stemmed, white and green parts chopped into ¼-inch pieces

1 cup shiitake mushrooms, stems removed and caps chopped into ¼-inch pieces

1 stalk celery, green part only, chopped into ¼-inch pieces

1 tablespoon oyster sauce

1 tablespoon soy sauce

1 teaspoon toasted sesame oil

¼ teaspoon ground black pepper

2 tablespoons water

1 bag (8 ounces) cole slaw or broccoli slaw mix

½ red bell pepper, seeded and cut into thin strips

½ pound shrimp, shelled, deveined and cut into ¼-inch pieces

3 tablespoons salted, dry roasted peanuts, coarsely chopped crushed

Hoisin sauce, to taste

10 to 15 leaves crisp romaine lettuce, white rib removed and patted dry

Fresh chives (optional)

Heat oil in small skillet over medium-high heat. Add meat and brown lightly on all sides about 4 to 5 minutes. Transfer to 4½-quart **CROCK-POT®** slow cooker. Add leeks, mushrooms and celery. Stir in oyster sauce, soy sauce, sesame oil, black pepper and water. Toss slaw and red pepper together and place in single layer on top of meat.

Cover and cook on LOW 4 to 5 hours or on HIGH 2 to 2½ hours or or until meat is cooked through. Stir in shrimp for last 20 minutes of cooking. When shrimp are pink and firm, remove mixture to large bowl. Add chopped peanuts and mix well.

To serve, spread about 1 teaspoon hoisin sauce on lettuce leaf. Add 1 to 2 tablespoons meat mixture and tightly roll like a cigar; secure by tying chives around rolled leaves. Alternatively, set out bowls of filling, hoisin and meat mixture for guests to roll themselves.

asian chicken fondue

SERVINGS: 6 TO 8 | PREP TIME: 30 MINUTES
LOW: ABOUT 5 HOURS

1	cup shiitake mushrooms, stems removed
2	cups chicken broth
1	tablespoon teriyaki sauce
1	small leek, white and green parts, cleaned, trimmed and chopped
1	head baby bok choy, trimmed and roughly chopped
1	tablespoon mirin
2	tablespoons oyster sauce
1	tablespoon canola oil
2	pounds boneless skinless chicken breast, cut into 1-inch cubes
1	cup peeled, seeded and cubed butternut squash
1	tablespoon cornstarch
2	tablespoons cold water
1	can (8 ounces) baby corn, drained
1	can (8 ounces) water chestnuts, drained

All specialty ingredients are available in the Asian foods aisle of your local grocer.

Combine mushrooms, chicken broth, teriyaki sauce, leek, bok choy, mirin, and oyster sauce in 4½-quart **CROCK-POT**® slow cooker. Cover and cook on LOW while following remaining instructions.

Heat oil in large skillet over medium-high heat. Season chicken with salt and pepper. Add to pan; cook without stirring until browned on bottom, about 4 minutes. Turn and brown other side. Stir into sauce in **CROCK-POT**® slow cooker. Stir in butternut squash.

Cover and continue cooking on LOW 4½ to 5 hours. Twenty minutes before end of cooking, stir cornstarch into cold water; set aside. Stir baby corn and water chestnuts into **CROCK-POT**® slow cooker then stir in cornstarch mixture. Cover and continue cooking on LOW. Serve with bamboo skewers, fondue forks or tongs so guests may serve themselves as desired. Broth may also be served in small soup bowls.

kashk-e bademjan (persian eggplant dip)

SERVINGS: 12 TO 16 | PREP TIME: 30 MINUTES
HIGH: 3½ TO 4 HOURS | LOW: 6 TO 8 HOURS

3   large eggplants (3½ pounds total), peeled and cut into 1-inch cubes

1   teaspoon salt

5   tablespoons extra-virgin olive oil, divided

2   onions, chopped

1   tablespoon dried mint

3   tablespoons Greek-style strained yogurt*

⅓   cup finely chopped walnuts

    Warm pita bread, cut into wedges

*Greek-style strained yogurt is yogurt from which much of the liquid has been drained before use. It is available in most major grocery stores, or to make your own, place ½ cup unflavored yogurt in a small colander lined with several layers of dampened cheesecloth. Suspend over a large bowl and refrigerate overnight.

Toss eggplant with salt in large bowl; transfer to large colander. Rest colander in large bowl or sink and let stand 1 hour at room temperature to drain.

Meanwhile, heat 1 tablespoon oil in large nonstick skillet over medium-high heat. Add onions and cook until lightly browned, 5 to 6 minutes, stirring occasionally. Transfer into 4½-quart **CROCK-POT®** slow cooker. Stir in eggplant. Cover and cook on LOW 6 to 8 hours or on HIGH 3½ to 4 hours or until eggplant is very soft.

Meanwhile, cook remaining 4 tablespoons oil and mint in small saucepan over low heat until very fragrant, about 15 minutes; cool.

Transfer eggplant and onions with slotted spoon to colander or fine mesh strainer and press out any excess liquid with back of spoon. Return to **CROCK-POT®** slow cooker and mash with fork. Stir in yogurt. Sprinkle with chopped walnuts and pour mint oil over top. Serve warm with pita bread.

TIP: Traditionally this dish is made with Kashk, an Iranian dairy product similar to sour cream and whey. Thick Greek-style strained yogurt is the closest substitute that is widely available in U.S. markets. "Bademjan" is the word for "eggplant" in Farsi, the language spoken in Iran.

channa chat
(indian-spiced snack mix)

SERVINGS: 6 TO 8 | PREP TIME: 40 MINUTES
HIGH: 3 HOURS | LOW: 6 HOURS

2	teaspoons canola oil
1	medium onion, finely chopped, divided
2	cloves garlic, minced
2	cans (15 ounces each) chickpeas, rinsed and drained
¼	cup vegetable broth or water
2	teaspoons tomato paste
¼	teaspoon ground cinnamon
¼	teaspoon ground cumin
¼	teaspoon black pepper
1	bay leaf
½	cup balsamic vinegar
1	tablespoons brown sugar
1	plum tomato, chopped
½	jalapeño pepper, stemmed and minced* or ¼ teaspoon ground red pepper (optional)
½	cup crisp rice cereal
3	tablespoons chopped fresh cilantro (optional)

*Jalapeño peppers can sting and irritate the skin, so wear rubber gloves when handling peppers and do not touch eyes.

Heat oil in small skillet over medium-high heat. Add one-half of onion and garlic. Reduce heat to medium and cook until soft, about 2 minutes. Transfer to 4½-quart CROCK-POT® slow cooker. Stir in chickpeas, vegetable broth, tomato paste, cinnamon, cumin, black pepper and bay leaf. Mix well.

Cover and cook on LOW 6 hours or on HIGH 3 hours.

Meanwhile, cook balsamic vinegar and brown sugar together in small saucepan over medium-low heat. Cook until vinegar is reduced by half and mixture becomes syrupy. Set aside.

When chickpeas are cooked, remove with slotted spoon and place in wide bowl. Allow to cool 15 minutes. Toss with tomato, remaining onion and jalapeño, if desired. Gently fold in crisp rice cereal and drizzle with balsamic syrup. Serve garnished with cilantro.

mini carnitas tacos

SERVINGS: 12 (36 MINI TACOS) | PREP TIME: 20 MINUTES
HIGH: 3 HOURS | LOW: 6 HOURS

1½ pounds boneless pork loin, cut into 1-inch cubes

1 onion, finely chopped

½ cup reduced-sodium chicken broth

1 tablespoon chili powder

2 teaspoons ground cumin

1 teaspoon dried oregano

½ teaspoon minced chipotle chile in adobo sauce

½ cup pico de gallo

2 tablespoons chopped fresh cilantro

½ teaspoon salt

12 (6-inch) flour or corn tortillas

¾ cup shredded sharp Cheddar cheese (optional)

3 tablespoons sour cream (optional)

Combine pork, onion, broth, chili powder, cumin, oregano and chipotle in 3½- to 4-quart **CROCK-POT**® slow cooker. Cover and cook on LOW 6 hours or on HIGH 3 hours or until pork is very tender. Pour off excess cooking liquid.

Shred pork with 2 forks; stir in pico de gallo, cilantro and salt. Cover and keep warm on LOW or WARM until serving.

Cut 3 circles from each tortilla with 2-inch biscuit cutter. Top each with some pork and garnish as desired with Cheddar cheese and sour cream. Serve warm.

TIP: Carnitas, or "little meats" in Spanish, are a festive way to spice up any gathering. Carnitas traditionally include a large amount of lard, but slow cooking makes the dish more healthful by eliminating the need to add lard, oil or fat, while keeping the meat tender and tasteful.

chicken liver pâté

SERVINGS: 8 TO 10 | PREP TIME: 15 MINUTES
LOW: 2 HOURS

PÂTÉ

1½   pounds chicken livers, trimmed of fat and membrane

1   small onion, thinly sliced

3   sprigs fresh thyme

2   cloves garlic, peeled and smashed

¼   teaspoon salt

1   tablespoon water

3   tablespoons cold butter, cut into 4 pieces

2   tablespoons heavy cream

2   tablespoons sherry

GARNISH

½   shallot, minced (optional)

2   tablespoons chopped fresh parsley (optional)

1   tablespoon sherry vinegar (optional)

⅛   teaspoon sugar

    Salt and black pepper to taste

    Melba toast or toast points

Rinse chicken livers and pat dry. Place in 4½-quart **CROCK-POT®** slow cooker. Add onion, thyme, garlic, salt and water. Cover and cook on LOW 2 hours.

Remove thyme springs from cooked livers and discard. Pour remaining ingredients from **CROCK-POT®** slow cooker into strainer and cool until just warm to the touch. Transfer to food processor and pulse just long enough to coarsely chop livers. Add butter one piece at a time, pulsing just enough after each addition to combine butter with liver pâté.

Add heavy cream and sherry and pulse once or twice more to combine. Transfer to serving bowl and serve immediately. Alternatively, transfer to a small loaf pan, pressing plastic wrap to surface of pâté. Refrigerate overnight, tightly wrapped in additional plastic wrap. Unmold pâté and slice to serve.

To garnish pâté (room temperature or refrigerated), stir together shallot, if desired, parsley, vinegar, sugar, salt and black pepper in small bowl. Set aside 5 minutes, then spoon over pâté. Serve with Melba toast or toast points.

stuffed baby bell peppers

SERVINGS: 16 TO 18 | PREP TIME: 45 MINUTES
HIGH: 2½ HOURS | LOW: 5 HOURS

1 tablespoon extra-virgin olive oil

½ medium onion, chopped

½ pound ground beef, chicken or turkey

½ cup cooked white rice

1 tablespoon dried dill weed

3 tablespoons chopped fresh parsley

1 tablespoon tomato paste, divided

2 tablespoons lemon juice

⅛ teaspoon black pepper

½ teaspoon salt

1 bag yellow and red baby bell peppers

¼ cup vegetable, chicken or beef broth

Heat oil in medium skillet over medium heat. Add onion and cook, stirring occasionally, until translucent.

Add ground meat and cook, stirring to break up meat, until cooked through and lightly browned. Drain meat and transfer to large bowl. Add rice, dill weed, parsley, 1½ teaspoons tomato paste, lemon juice, pepper and salt. Mix well until well combined. Set aside.

Cut small slit in the side of each baby bell pepper and run under cold water to wash out seeds. Fill each pepper with 2 to 3 teaspoons seasoned meat. Place peppers in 4½-quart **CROCK-POT®** slow cooker, slit side up. Add broth and remaining tomato paste. Cover and cook on LOW 5 hours or on HIGH 2½ hours. Serve hot.

apricot & brie dip

SERVINGS: 8 TO 12 (3 CUPS TOTAL) | PREP TIME: 10 MINUTES
HIGH: 1¼ TO 1½ HOURS

½ cup dried apricots, finely chopped

⅓ cup plus 1 tablespoon apricot preserves, divided

¼ cup apple juice

1 (2-pound) brie, rind removed, cut into cubes

Bread rusks, crackers or crudité for dipping

Combine dried apricots, ⅓ cup apricot preserves and apple juice in 3½- to 4-quart **CROCK-POT®** slow cooker. Cover and cook on HIGH 40 minutes. Stir in brie and cook 30 to 40 minutes longer or until melted. Stir in remaining 1 tablespoon preserves. Turn **CROCK-POT®** slow cooker to LOW and serve with bread rusks, crackers or crudité.

south pacific pork ribs

SERVINGS: 4 TO 6 | PREP TIME: 40 MINUTES
HIGH: 5 TO 6 HOURS | LOW: 8 TO 10 HOURS

2 tablespoons canola oil, divided

3½ to 4 pounds pork loin riblets (about 20 riblets)

Salt and black pepper

1 onion, chopped

1 can (20 ounces) pineapple chunks in 100% pineapple juice, drained, reserving about 1 cup juice

¼ cup packed brown sugar

¼ cup all-purpose flour

¼ cup ketchup

¼ cup vinegar

½ cup water

1 tablespoon soy sauce

Heat 1 tablespoon oil in large skillet over medium-high heat. Season riblets with salt and pepper. Working in batches, brown riblets in hot oil, turning to brown both sides. Transfer to 3½-quart **CROCK-POT®** slow cooker as ribs are done. Halfway through browning, add remaining tablespoon oil to pan. When all riblets are finished browning, stir onion into hot pan. Cook until softened, 3 to 5 minutes.

Meanwhile, whisk together pineapple juice and flour until well blended; set aside. Stir ketchup, brown sugar, vinegar, water and soy sauce into pan. Stir in juice mixture until well combined. Simmer until thickened. Add pineapple chunks and pour sauce over ribs.

Cover and cook ribs on LOW 8 to 10 hours or on HIGH 5 to 6 hours or until tender.

apricot & brie dip

thai chicken wings

SERVINGS: 8 | PREP TIME: 20 MINUTES
HIGH: 3 TO 3½ HOURS | LOW: 6 TO 7 HOURS

1 tablespoon peanut oil

5 pounds chicken wings, tips removed and split at the joint

½ cup coconut milk

1 tablespoon Thai green curry paste

1 tablespoon fish sauce

1 tablespoon sugar

¾ cup prepared spicy peanut sauce

Heat oil in large nonstick skillet over medium-high heat. Add chicken wings and brown in several batches, about 6 minutes per batch. Transfer wings to 4½-quart **CROCK-POT®** slow cooker as they are browned.

Stir in coconut milk, curry paste, fish sauce and sugar. Cover and cook on LOW 6 to 7 hours or on HIGH 3 to 3½ hours or until tender. Drain off cooking liquid and carefully stir in peanut sauce before serving.

stewed fig & blue cheese dip

SERVINGS: 6 TO 8 | PREP TIME: 15 MINUTES
HIGH: 1 TO 1½ HOURS

1 tablespoon olive oil

1 medium onion, chopped

½ cup port wine

1 package (6 ounces) dried calimyrna figs, finely chopped

½ cup orange juice

½ cup crumbled blue cheese, divided

1 tablespoon unsalted butter

Heat oil in small nonstick skillet over medium-high heat. Add onion and cook, stirring occasionally, until light golden, 7 to 8 minutes. Stir in port and bring to a boil; cook 1 minute. Transfer to 1½-quart **CROCK-POT®** slow cooker; stir in figs and orange juice.

Cover and cook on HIGH until figs are plump and tender, 1 to 1½ hours. Stir in ¼ cup blue cheese and butter. Sprinkle with remaining blue cheese and serve.

thai chicken wings

bagna cauda

¾ cup olive oil

6 tablespoons butter, softened

12 anchovy fillets, drained

6 cloves garlic, peeled

⅛ teaspoon red pepper flakes

Assorted foods for dipping such as endive spears, cauliflower florettes, cucumber spears, carrot sticks, zucchini spears, red bell pepper pieces, sugar snap peas or crusty Italian or French bread slices

Place olive oil, butter, anchovies, garlic and pepper flakes in food processor and process until quite smooth, about 30 seconds. Scrape mixture into 2-½ to 4-quart **CROCK-POT®** slow cooker. Cover and cook on LOW 2 hours or on HIGH 1 hour or until mixture is hot. Turn to LOW and serve with assorted dippers.

TIP: Bagna cauda is a warm Italian dip similar to the more famous fondue. The name is derived from "bagno caldo," meaning "warm bath" in Italian. This dip should be kept warm while serving, just like you would fondue.

chorizo & queso fundido

2 cured chorizo sausages (about 3½ ounces total), finely chopped*

8 ounces Monterey Jack cheese, cubed

8 ounces cream cheese, cubed

8 ounces processed cheese spread, cubed

8 ounces Cheddar cheese, cubed

1 tablespoon Worcestershire sauce

Tortilla chips

There are two styles of chorizo widely available in most major supermarkets. Mexican-style, or uncured, chorizo is typically sold in ½- or 1-pound refrigerated packages. Spanish-style, or cured, chorizo is sold in links of varying sizes held together by their casings.

Combine chorizo, cheeses, and Worcestershire sauce in 3½- to 4-quart **CROCK-POT®** slow cooker. Cover and on HIGH 1 to 1½ hours or until cheese looks very soft; whisk to blend and keep warm on LOW or WARM. Serve with tortilla chips.

TIP: In Spanish, queso fundido means "melted cheese," which precisely describes this dish. For a more authentic taste, replace some of the cheeses with Mexican cheeses such as queso fresco, chihuahua or cotija.

moroccan-spiced chicken wings

SERVINGS: 8 | PREP TIME: 20 MINUTES
HIGH: 3 TO 3½ HOURS | LOW: 6 TO 7 HOURS

¼ cup orange juice

3 tablespoons tomato paste

2 teaspoons ground cumin

1 teaspoon curry powder

1 teaspoon ground turmeric

½ teaspoon ground cinnamon

½ teaspoon ground ginger

1 teaspoon salt

1 tablespoon olive oil

5 pounds chicken wings, tips removed and split at joints

Stir together orange juice, tomato paste, cumin, curry, turmeric, cinnamon, ginger and salt in large bowl; set aside.

Heat oil in large nonstick skillet over medium-high heat. Add wings and brown in several batches, about 6 minutes per batch. Transfer wings to bowl with sauce as they are cooked. When all wings are cooked, toss well to coat.

Place wings in 4½-quart **CROCK-POT®** slow cooker. Cover and cook on LOW 6 to 7 hours or on HIGH 3 to 3½ hours or until tender.

bacon-wrapped fingerling potatoes with thyme

SERVINGS: 4 TO 6 | PREP TIME 45 MINUTES
HIGH: 3 HOURS

1   pound fingerling potatoes, washed, patted dry and stem ends trimmed

1   tablespoons minced fresh thyme

2   tablespoons olive oil

½   teaspoon black pepper

¼   teaspoon paprika

½   pound package fatty bacon strips

¼   cup chicken broth

Toss potatoes with thyme, olive oil, black pepper and paprika in large bowl. Set aside.

Cut each bacon slice in half lengthwise; wrap half slice bacon tightly around each potato.

Heat large skillet over medium heat; add potatoes. Reduce heat to medium-low and cook until lightly browned and some bacon fat has rendered out. Bacon should sear "shut" around potatoes.

Place potatoes in 4½-quart **CROCK-POT®** slow cooker. Add chicken broth, cover and cook on HIGH 3 hours. Remove from **CROCK-POT®** slow cooker and serve.

TIP: This appetizer can be made even more eye-catching with rare varieties of potatoes. Many interesting types of small potatoes can be found at farmers' markets. Purple potatoes, about the size of fingerling potatoes, can add some more color and spunk to this dish.

International
Specialties

spanish paella with chicken & sausage

SERVINGS: 4 | PREP TIME: 25 MINUTES
HIGH: 3 TO 4 HOURS | LOW: 6 TO 8 HOURS

1 tablespoon olive oil

4 chicken thighs, about 2 pounds total

1 medium onion, chopped

1 clove garlic, minced

1 pound hot smoked sausage, sliced into rounds

1 can (14½ ounces) stewed tomatoes, undrained

4 cups chicken broth

1 pinch saffron, optional

1 cup arborio rice

½ cup frozen peas, thawed

Heat oil in large skillet over medium-high heat until hot. Add chicken pieces in batches and brown well on all sides. Transfer chicken to 5-quart **CROCK-POT®** slow cooker as it browns.

Add onion to same skillet and cook until translucent. Stir in garlic, sausage, tomatoes and chicken broth. Stir in saffron and rice. Pour over chicken. Cover and cook on LOW 6 to 8 hours or on HIGH 3 to 4 hours or until chicken is fully cooked and rice is tender.

Remove chicken pieces to serving platter and fluff rice with fork. Stir in peas. Spoon rice onto platter with chicken.

chicken & mushroom fettuccini alfredo

SERVINGS: 6 TO 8 | PREP TIME: 20 MINUTES
HIGH: 2 TO 2½ HOURS | LOW: 4 TO 5 HOURS

1½ pounds chicken breast tenders

2 packages (8 ounces each) cremini mushrooms, cut into thirds

½ teaspoon salt

¼ teaspoon black pepper

¼ teaspoon garlic powder

2 packages (8 ounces each) cream cheese, cut into chunks

1 cup (2 sticks) butter, cut into pieces

1½ cups grated Parmesan cheese, plus additional for garnish

1½ cups whole milk

1 package (1 pound) fettuccini

Spray inside of 5-quart **CROCK-POT®** slow cooker with nonstick cooking spray. Arrange chicken in single layer in bottom of **CROCK-POT®** slow cooker. Top with mushrooms. Sprinkle salt, black pepper and garlic powder over mushrooms.

Stir together cream cheese, butter, Parmesan cheese and milk in medium saucepan over medium heat. Whisk constantly until smooth and heated through. Pour over mushrooms, pushing down any that float to surface. Cover and cook on LOW 4 to 5 hours or on HIGH 2 to 2½ hours.

Cook fettuccini in boiling, salted water according to package directions. Drain. Add fettuccine to Alfredo sauce and toss gently to combine. Serve with additional Parmesan.

basque chicken with peppers

SERVINGS: 4 TO 6 | PREP TIME: 15 MINUTES
HIGH: 4 HOURS | LOW: 5 TO 6 HOURS

1	whole chicken (4 pounds), cut into 8 pieces
	Salt and black pepper
1½	tablespoons olive oil
1	onion, chopped
1	medium green pepper, seeded and cut into strips
1	medium yellow pepper, seeded and cut into strips
1	medium red pepper, seeded and cut into strips
8	ounces small brown mushrooms, halved
2	cloves garlic, minced
½	cup Rioja wine
1	can (14½ ounces) stewed tomatoes
3	ounces tomato paste
½	cup chicken broth
1	sprig fresh marjoram
1	teaspoon salt
½	teaspoon black pepper
1	teaspoon smoked paprika
4	ounces diced prosciutto
	Cooked rice or rice pilaf

Rinse chicken pieces and pat dry. Season with salt and pepper.

Heat olive oil until hot in large skillet over medium-high heat. Add chicken in batches and brown well on all sides. As chicken pieces brown place them in 4½-quart **CROCK-POT**® slow cooker.

Reduce heat under skillet to medium-low and stir in onions. Cook until softened, stirring frequently, about 3 minutes. Add peppers and mushrooms to skillet and cook 3 minutes more. Add all remaining ingredients except prosciutto and rice to skillet and bring to simmer. Simmer 3 to 4 minutes and pour over chicken. Cover and cook on LOW 5 to 6 hours or on HIGH 4 hours or until chicken is tender.

Remove chicken pieces to deep platter or wide serving bowl with tongs. Ladle vegetables and sauce over chicken. Sprinkle prosciutto over top. Serve with cooked rice.

asian beef
with mandarin oranges

SERVINGS: 6 | PREP TIME: 25 MINUTES
HIGH: 5 TO 6 HOURS | LOW: 10 HOURS

2	tablespoons vegetable oil
2	pounds boneless beef chuck, cut into ½-inch strips
1	small onion, thinly sliced
⅓	cup soy sauce
¼	teaspoon salt
2	teaspoons minced fresh ginger
1	small green bell pepper, sliced
1	package (about 3 ounces) shiitake mushrooms, sliced
1	bunch bok choy, cleaned and chopped
1	can (5 ounces) sliced water chestnuts, drained
2	tablespoons corn starch
1	can (11 ounces) mandarin oranges, drained and syrup reserved
2	cups beef broth
6	cups steamed rice

Heat vegetable oil over medium-high heat. Add beef, in batches if necessary, and cook, turning to brown all sides. Transfer beef to 4½-quart **CROCK-POT®** slow cooker as it is browned.

Add onion to same skillet. Stir over medium heat until softened. Add next soy sauce, salt, ginger, green pepper, mushrooms, bok choy and water chestnuts and cook until bok choy is wilted, about 5 minutes. Spoon mixture over beef.

Whisk together corn starch and reserved mandarin orange syrup in medium bowl. Stir in beef broth and pour over ingredients in **CROCK-POT®** slow cooker. Cover and cook on LOW 10 hours or on HIGH 5 to 6 hours or until beef is tender.

Stir in mandarin oranges. Spoon steamed rice into shallow serving bowl and spoon beef over rice.

chinese pork tenderloin

SERVINGS: 8 | PREP TIME: 15 MINUTES
HIGH: 4 TO 5 HOURS | LOW: 6 TO 7 HOURS

2   pork tenderloins (about 2 pounds total)

1   green bell pepper, seeded and cut into ½-inch dice

1   red bell pepper, seeded and cut into ½-inch dice

1   medium onion, thinly sliced

2   carrots, peeled and thinly sliced

1   jar (15 ounces) sweet and sour sauce

1   tablespoon soy sauce

½   teaspoon red pepper sauce

    Cooked white rice

    Chopped fresh cilantro or parsley (optional)

Cut pork into 1-inch cubes and place in 5- or 6-quart **CROCK-POT®** slow cooker.

Add diced peppers, onion, carrots, sweet and sour sauce, soy sauce and hot pepper sauce. Stir just to combine. Cover and cook on LOW 6 to 7 hours or on HIGH 4 to 5 hours. Stir again just before serving, Serve over hot rice and sprinkle with chopped cilantro.

chicken tangier

SERVINGS: 8 | PREP TIME: 15 MINUTES
HIGH: 4 TO 5 HOURS | LOW: 7 TO 8 HOURS

2   tablespoons dried oregano

2   teaspoons seasoning salt

2   teaspoons puréed garlic

¼   teaspoon black pepper

8   skinless chicken thighs (about 3 pounds)

1   lemon, thinly sliced

½   cup dry white wine

2   tablespoons olive oil

1   cup pitted prunes

¼   cup currants or raisins

½   cup pitted green olives

2   tablespoons capers

    Cooked noodles or rice

    Chopped fresh parsley or cilantro (optional)

Stir together oregano, salt, garlic and pepper in small bowl. Rub onto chicken, being certain to coat all sides.

Coat inside of 5- or 6-quart **CROCK-POT®** slow cooker with nonstick cooking spray. Arrange chicken inside, tucking lemon slices between pieces. Pour wine over chicken and sprinkle with olive oil. Add prunes, currants, olives and capers. Cover and cook on LOW 7 to 8 hours or on HIGH 4 to 5 hours.

Serve over cooked noodles or rice and sprinkle with parsley.

TIP: It may seem like a lot, but this recipe really does call for 2 tablespoons dried oregano in order to more accurately represent the powerfully seasoned flavors of Morocco.

sesame chicken

SERVINGS: 4 TO 6 | PREP TIME: 25 MINUTES
HIGH: 3 TO 4 HOURS | LOW: 7 TO 8 HOURS

4 chicken legs (or 4 thighs and 4 drumsticks)

4 bone-in chicken breasts

1 cup rice flour

8 teaspoons sesame seeds

Salt and black pepper

Vegetable oil

1 cup chicken broth

½ cup chopped celery

¼ cup chopped onion

1 teaspoon dried tarragon

¼ cup cornstarch

¼ cup water

1½ cups sour cream

Cut through joints to separate thighs and drumsticks. Split breasts in half. Mix rice flour, sesame seeds, salt and pepper in medium bowl. Dip chicken pieces in mixture to coat.

Heat oil in skillet over medium heat until hot. Brown chicken on all sides, turning as it browns. Transfer to paper towel-lined plate with slotted spoon to drain excess fat. Place in 4½-quart **CROCK-POT**® slow cooker.

Add broth, celery, onion and tarragon. Cover; cook on LOW 7 to 8 hours or on HIGH 3 to 4 hours.

Turn CROCK-POT® slow cooker to HIGH. Combine cornstarch and water in small bowl. Add sour cream. Mix well to combine. Add to **CROCK-POT**® slow cooker. Stir gently to combine. Cover; cook 15 to 20 minutes or until thickened.

saffron-scented shrimp paella

SERVINGS: 4 TO 6 | PREP TIME: 40 MINUTES

HIGH: ¾ TO 1¼ HOURS

3	tablespoons olive oil, divided
1½	cups chopped onions
4	cloves garlic, thinly sliced
	Salt, to taste
1	cup roasted red bell pepper, diced
1	cup chopped tomato
1	bay leaf
1	large pinch saffron
1	cup white wine
8	cups chicken broth
4	cups uncooked white rice
25	large shrimp, peeled, deveined and cleaned
	White pepper

Heat 2 tablespoons oil in large skillet over medium heat until hot. Add onions, garlic and salt. Cook and stir until translucent, about 5 minutes. Add bell pepper, tomato, bay leaf and saffron. Cook and stir until heated through. Add wine. Continue cooking until liquid has reduced by half.

Add broth. Bring to a simmer. Adjust seasonings, if desired, and stir in rice. Transfer to 4½-quart **CROCK-POT®** slow cooker. Cover; cook on HIGH 30 minutes to 1 hour or until rice has absorbed all of liquid.

Toss shrimp in remaining 1 tablespoon olive oil and season with salt and white pepper. Place shrimp on rice in **CROCK-POT®** slow cooker. Cover; cook about 10 minutes or until shrimp are just cooked through.

asian pork ribs with spicy noodles

SERVINGS: 4 | PREP TIME: 20 MINUTES
HIGH: 5 TO 6 HOURS | LOW: 8 TO 10 HOURS

1   can (14 ounces) beef broth

½   cup water

¼   cup rice wine vinegar

1   ounce (2-inch piece) fresh ginger, peeled and grated

1   cup (about 1 ounce) dried sliced shiitake mushrooms

¼   teaspoon red pepper flakes

1   tablespoon Chinese 5-spice powder

1   teaspoon ground ginger

1   teaspoon chili powder

1   tablespoon toasted (dark) sesame oil

2   full racks pork back ribs (about 4 pounds total)

¾   cup hoisin sauce, divided

1   pound (16 ounces) thin spaghetti, cooked according to package directions

¼   cup thinly sliced green onions

¼   cup chopped fresh cilantro

Stir together beef broth, water, rice wine vinegar, grated ginger, shiitake mushrooms and red pepper flakes in a 6-quart **CROCK-POT®** slow cooker.

Stir together 5-spice powder, ground ginger, chili powder and sesame oil to form a paste. Blot ribs dry with paper towels. Rub both sides with spice paste and brush with half of hoisin sauce.

Place ribs in **CROCK-POT®** slow cooker with prepared cooking liquid (do not stir). Cover and cook on LOW 8 to 10 hours or on HIGH 5 to 6 hours or until meat is tender when pierced with a fork. Remove ribs to platter and brush lightly with remaining hoisin sauce. Keep warm until serving. Meanwhile, skim off any fat from cooking liquid.

Place warm spaghetti in shallow bowl. Ladle some hot broth over spaghetti and sprinkle with green onions and cilantro. Slice ribs and serve over pasta.

sweet & spicy pork picadillo

SERVINGS: 4 | PREP TIME: 15 MINUTES
HIGH: 3½ HOURS | LOW: 5½ HOURS

1 tablespoon olive oil

1 yellow onion, cut into ¼-inch dice

2 cloves garlic, minced

1 pound boneless pork country-style ribs, trimmed of excess fat and cut into 1-inch cubes

1 can (14½ ounces) diced tomatoes, undrained

3 tablespoons cider vinegar

2 chipotle peppers (canned in adobo), chopped

½ cup raisins, chopped

½ teaspoon cumin

½ teaspoon ground cinnamon

Salt and black pepper

Heat olive oil in skillet over medium-low heat until hot. Cook and stir onion and garlic until translucent, about 4 minutes.

Add pork to skillet and brown. Transfer to 4½-quart **CROCK-POT®** slow cooker.

Combine tomatoes, vinegar, chipotle peppers, raisins, cumin and cinnamon in medium bowl. Pour over pork. Cover; cook on LOW 5 hours or on HIGH 3 hours or until pork is fork tender.

Shred pork using 2 forks. Cook 30 minutes longer. Adjust seasonings with salt and pepper before serving, if desired.

moroccan-style lamb shoulder chops with couscous

SERVINGS: 4 | PREP TIME: 15 MINUTES
HIGH: 3½ TO 4 HOURS

4   lamb blade chops (about 2½ pounds)

     Salt and black pepper

1   tablespoon olive oil

1   onion, chopped

1   clove garlic, minced

1   teaspoon grated fresh ginger

¼   teaspoon ground cinnamon

½   teaspoon ground turmeric

½   teaspoon salt

¼   teaspoon black pepper

1   bay leaf

1   can (14½ ounces) diced tomatoes, undrained

1   cup canned chickpeas, rinsed and drained

½   cup water

2   tablespoons lemon juice

     Hot couscous

     Lemon wedges (optional)

Coat inside of 5- to 6-quart **CROCK-POT®** slow cooker with nonstick cooking spray. Season lamb chops with salt and pepper to taste. Heat oil in large skillet over medium-high heat until hot. Add lamb chops and brown on all sides. Transfer to **CROCK-POT®** slow cooker.

Add onion to skillet. Cook and stir 2 to 3 minutes or until translucent. Add garlic, ginger, cinnamon, turmeric, salt, pepper and bay leaf. Cook and stir 30 seconds longer. Stir in tomatoes with juice, chickpeas, water and lemon juice. Simmer 2 minutes. Pour mixture over lamb. Cover; cook on HIGH 3½ to 4 hours or until lamb is tender.

Add salt and pepper, if desired. Serve lamb chops with sauce and vegetables over couscous. Serve with lemon wedges, if desired.

fall-apart pork roast with mole

SERVINGS: 6 | PREP TIME: 10 TO 15 MINUTES
HIGH: 3 TO 4 HOURS | LOW: 7 TO 8 HOURS

⅔ cup whole almonds

⅔ cup raisins

3 tablespoons vegetable oil, divided

½ cup chopped onions

4 cloves garlic, chopped

2¾ pounds lean boneless pork shoulder roast, well trimmed

1 can (14½ ounces) diced fire-roasted tomatoes or diced tomatoes, undrained

1 cup cubed bread, any variety

½ cup chicken broth

2 ounces Mexican chocolate, chopped

2 tablespoons chipotle peppers in adobo sauce, chopped

1 teaspoon salt

Fresh cilantro, coarsely chopped (optional)

Heat large skillet over medium-high heat until hot. Add almonds and toast 3 to 4 minutes, stirring frequently, until fragrant. Add raisins. Cook 1 to 2 minutes longer, stirring constantly, until raisins begin to plump. Place half of almond mixture in large mixing bowl. Reserve remaining half for garnish.

Heat 1 tablespoon oil in large skillet. Add onions and garlic. Cook and stir 2 to 3 minutes until softened. Add to almond mixture in bowl; set aside.

Heat remaining oil in same skillet. Add pork roast and brown on all sides, about 5 to 7 minutes. Transfer to 4½-quart CROCK-POT® slow cooker.

Combine tomatoes with juice, bread, broth, chocolate, chipotle peppers and salt with almond mixture. Purée mixture in blender in 2 or 3 batches. Pour over pork roast in CROCK-POT® slow cooker.

Cover; cook on LOW 7 to 8 hours or on HIGH 3 to 4 hours or until pork is done. Remove pork roast from CROCK-POT® slow cooker. Whisk sauce until smooth before spooning over pork roast. Garnish with reserved almond mixture and chopped cilantro.

cod tapenade

SERVINGS: 4 | PREP TIME: 20 MINUTES

HIGH: 1 HOUR

4   cod fillets, or other firm-fleshed
    white fish (2 to 3 pounds
    total)

    Salt and black pepper

2   lemons, thinly sliced

    Tapenade (recipe follows)

TAPENADE

½   pound pitted kalamata olives

2   tablespoons anchovy paste

2   tablespoons capers, drained

1   clove garlic

⅛   teaspoon ground red pepper

¼   teaspoon grated orange zest

2   tablespoons chopped fresh
    thyme or flat-leaf parsley

4   tablespoons olive oil

Season fish with salt and pepper.

Arrange half lemon slices in bottom of 4½-quart **CROCK-POT®** slow cooker. Top with fish. Cover fish with remaining lemon slices. Cover. Cook on HIGH 1 hour or until fish is just cooked through (actual time depends on thickness of fish).

Remove fish to serving plates; discard lemon. Top with Tapenade.

TO PREPARE TAPENADE: Place all ingredients except oil in food processor. Pulse to roughly chop. Add oil and pulse briefly to form a chunky paste.

TIP: In a hurry? Substitute store-brought tapenade for homemade!

chicken parmesan with eggplant

SERVINGS: 6 TO 8 | PREP TIME: 30 MINUTES
HIGH: 2 TO 4 HOURS | LOW: 6 HOURS

6	boneless, skinless chicken breasts
2	eggs
2	teaspoons salt
2	teaspoons black pepper
2	cups Italian bread crumbs
½	cup olive oil
½	cup (1 stick) butter
2	small eggplants, cut into ¾-inch-thick slices
1½	cups grated Parmesan cheese
2½	cups tomato-basil sauce
1	pound sliced or shredded mozzarella cheese

Slice chicken breasts in half lengthwise. Cut each half lengthwise again into 4 (¾-inch) slices.

Combine eggs, salt and pepper in medium bowl. Place bread crumbs in separate bowl or on plate. Dip chicken in egg mixture, then coat in bread crumbs.

Heat oil and butter in skillet over medium heat until hot. Brown breaded chicken on all sides, turning as pieces brown. Transfer to paper towel-lined plate to drain excess oil.

Arrange eggplant in single layer on bottom of 4½-quart **CROCK-POT®** slow cooker. Add ¾ cup Parmesan cheese and 1¼ cups sauce. Arrange chicken on sauce. Add remaining Parmesan cheese and sauce. Top with mozzarella cheese. Cover; cook on LOW 6 hours or on HIGH 2 to 4 hours.

chicken saltimbocca-style

SERVINGS: 6 | PREP TIME: 25 MINUTES
HIGH: 2 TO 3 HOURS | LOW: 5 TO 7 HOURS

6   boneless, skinless chicken
     breasts

12 slices prosciutto

12 slices provolone cheese

½   cup all-purpose flour

½   cup grated Parmesan cheese

2   teaspoons salt

2   teaspoons black pepper
     Olive oil

2   cans (10¾ ounces each)
     condensed cream of
     mushroom soup, undiluted

¾   cup white wine (optional)

1   teaspoon ground sage

Split each chicken breast into 2 thin pieces. Place between 2 pieces of waxed paper or plastic wrap. Pound until ⅓-inch thick. Place 1 slice prosciutto and 1 slice provolone on each chicken piece and roll up. Secure with toothpicks.

Combine flour, Parmesan cheese, salt and pepper, and place on plate. Dredge chicken in flour mixture. Reserve excess flour mixture.

Heat oil in skillet over medium heat until hot. Brown chicken on both sides, turning as it browns. Transfer to 4½-quart **CROCK-POT®** slow cooker. Add soup, wine, if desired, and sage. Cover; cook on LOW 5 to 7 hours or on HIGH 2 to 3 hours.

To thicken sauce, stir in 2 to 3 tablespoons leftover flour mixture and cook 15 minutes before serving.

asian ginger beef over bok choy

SERVINGS: 6 TO 8 | PREP TIME: 15 MINUTES
HIGH: 3 TO 4 HOURS | LOW: 7 TO 8 HOURS

2 tablespoons peanut oil

1½ pounds boneless beef chuck roast, cut into 1-inch pieces

3 green onions, cut into ½-inch slices

6 cloves garlic, chopped

1 cup chicken broth

½ cup water

¼ cup soy sauce

2 teaspoons ground ginger

1 teaspoon Asian chili paste

9 ounces fresh udon noodles or vermicelli, cooked and drained

3 cups bok choy, trimmed, washed and cut into 1-inch pieces

½ cup minced fresh cilantro

Heat oil in large skillet over medium-high heat until hot. Sear beef on all sides in batches to prevent crowding, turning each piece as it browns. Sear last batch of beef with onions and garlic.

Transfer to 5- to 6-quart **CROCK-POT**® slow cooker. Add broth, water, soy sauce, ginger and chili paste. Stir well to combine. Cover; cook on LOW 7 to 8 hours or on HIGH 3 to 4 hours or until beef is very tender.

Just before serving, turn **CROCK-POT**® slow cooker to HIGH. Add noodles to **CROCK-POT**® slow cooker and stir well. Add bok choy and stir again. Heat on HIGH until bok choy is tender-crisp, about 15 minutes.

Garnish beef with cilantro and serve while hot.

golden duck

1   duck, split in half lengthwise
    (3 to 4 pounds)

1   can (12 ounces) dried apricots

¼   cup honey

2   tablespoons grated orange
    peel

2   tablespoons soy sauce

½   teaspoon seasoned salt

¼   cup water

2   tablespoons cornstarch

3   cans (12 ounces each) sliced
    cling peaches, drained and
    juice reserved

2   bananas, peeled and cut into
    ½-inch slices

Place duck, split side down, in bottom of 4½-quart **CROCK-POT®** slow cooker. Poke holes in duck skin with fork.

Combine apricots, honey, orange peel, soy sauce and seasoned salt in large bowl. Pour evenly over duck breast. Cover; cook on LOW 7 to 8 hours or on HIGH 3 to 4 hours or until tender (internal temperature of 185°F).

Transfer duck to cutting board. Pour remaining glaze into saucepan. Combine water and cornstarch. Stir into glaze and add reserved peach juice. Cook and stir glaze until thickened. Add peaches and bananas. Serve over duck.

braised pork shanks with israeli couscous

SERVINGS: 4 | PREP TIME: 40 MINUTES
HIGH: 3 HOURS

4   bone-in pork shanks, skin removed (about 1½ pounds total)

Coarse salt and black pepper, to taste

1   cup olive oil

4   large carrots, peeled and sliced diagonally into 1-inch segments, divided

4   stalks celery, sliced diagonally into 1-inch segments, divided

1   Spanish onion, peeled and quartered

4   cloves garlic, peeled and mashed

4   to 6 cups low-sodium chicken broth

2   cups dry white wine

¼   cup tomato paste

¼   cup distilled white vinegar

2   tablespoons mustard oil* (optional)

1   tablespoon whole black peppercorns

Israeli couscous (cooked according to package directions)

Mustard oil is available at Middle Eastern specialty shops or in the supermarket ethnic foods aisle.

Season shanks with salt and pepper. Heat oil in large skillet over medium heat until hot. Brown shanks on all sides, turning as they brown. Transfer to 4½-quart **CROCK-POT®** slow cooker.

Pour off all but 2 tablespoons oil from skillet. Add half of carrots, half of celery, onion and garlic. Cook and stir over medium-low heat until vegetables are soft but not brown, about 5 minutes. Transfer to **CROCK-POT®** slow cooker.

Add broth, wine, tomato paste, vinegar, mustard oil, if desired, and peppercorns. Bring to a boil, stirring and scraping up any browned bits in bottom of pan. Pour over shanks. Cover; cook on HIGH 2 hours, turning shanks every 20 minutes.

Remove shanks. Strain cooking liquid and discard solids. Return cooking liquid to **CROCK-POT®** slow cooker. Add remaining carrots and celery, and return shanks to **CROCK-POT®** slow cooker. Cover; cook on HIGH 1 hour.

To check shanks for doneness: remove one and place it on a plate. Meat should be very soft but still attached to bone.

To serve, add precooked couscous to **CROCK-POT®** slow cooker to reheat, 3 to 4 minutes. Using a slotted spoon, place couscous, carrots and celery in shallow bowls. Place shank on top and spoon one-fourth of cooking liquid into bowl.

mediterranean lamb shanks

SERVINGS: 6 | PREP TIME: 30 MINUTES
HIGH: 4½ TO 6½ HOURS | LOW: 7½ TO 9½ HOURS

3   pounds lamb shanks

   Salt and black pepper

   All-purpose flour, as needed

2   tablespoons olive oil

1   medium red onion, chopped

2   cloves garlic, minced

2   cups red wine

1   medium eggplant, peeled and cut into ½-inch cubes

1   large red bell pepper, cored, seeded and sliced

1   large tomato, seeded and chopped

1   teaspoon dried thyme

½   teaspoon dried rosemary

2   cinnamon sticks

½   cup kalamata olives, pitted

2   tablespoons minced flat-leaf parsley

Season lamb on both sides with salt and pepper, then lightly coat with flour. Heat oil in skillet over medium heat until hot. Sear lamb on all sides, 1 to 2 minutes per side, turning as it browns. Transfer to 4½-quart **CROCK-POT**® slow cooker.

Add onion and garlic to skillet. Cook and stir 3 to 4 minutes or until onions soften. Transfer to **CROCK-POT**® slow cooker.

Add wine, eggplant, bell pepper, tomato, thyme, rosemary and cinnamon sticks to **CROCK-POT**® slow cooker. Stir well to combine. Cover; cook on LOW 7½ to 9½ hours or on HIGH 4½ to 6½ hours or until meat is tender.

Remove cinnamon sticks before serving. Garnish with olives and parsley.

german-style bratwurst

4   pounds bratwurst

2   pounds sauerkraut, drained

6   apples, peeled, cored and
      thinly sliced

1   white onion, thinly sliced

1   teaspoon caraway seed

    Freshly ground black pepper

5   bottles (12 ounces each) any
      German-style beer

Combine all ingredients in 4½-quart **CROCK-POT®** slow cooker. Cover; cook on LOW 6 to 8 hours or on HIGH 3 to 4 hours or until done.

Easy Sides

lemon-mint red potatoes

SERVINGS: 4 | PREP TIME: 25 MINUTES
HIGH: 4 HOURS | LOW: 7 HOURS

2   pounds new potatoes

3   tablespoons extra-virgin olive oil

¾   teaspoon dried Greek seasoning or dried oregano leaves

¼   teaspoon garlic powder

1   teaspoon salt

¼   teaspoon black pepper

2   tablespoons lemon juice

1   teaspoon grated lemon peel

2   tablespoons butter

¼   cup chopped fresh mint leaves, divided

Coat inside of 6-quart **CROCK-POT®** slow cooker with nonstick cooking spray. Add potatoes and oil, stirring gently to coat. Sprinkle with Greek seasoning, garlic powder, salt and pepper. Cover and cook on LOW 7 hours or on HIGH 4 hours.

Stir in lemon juice, lemon peel, butter and 2 tablespoons mint. Stir until butter is completely melted. Cover and cook 15 minutes to allow flavors to blend. Sprinkle with remaining mint.

TIP: It's easy to prepare this recipe ahead of time; simply follow instructions as listed and then turn off heat and let stand at room temperature for up to two hours. Reheat or serve at room temperature.

asiago & asparagus risotto-style rice

SERVINGS: 4 | PREP TIME: 20 MINUTES
HIGH: 2½ HOURS

2 cups chopped onion

1 cup uncooked converted rice

2 medium garlic cloves, minced

1 can (14½ ounces) chicken broth

½ pound asparagus spears, trimmed and broken into 1-inch pieces

1 to 1¼ cups half-and-half, divided

½ cup (about 4 ounces) shredded Asiago cheese, plus more for garnish

¼ cup (½ stick) butter, cut into small pieces

2 ounces pine nuts or slivered almonds, toasted

1 teaspoon salt

Combine onion, rice, garlic and broth in 3½- to 4-quart **CROCK-POT®** slow cooker. Stir until well blended; cover and cook 2 hours on HIGH or until rice is done.

Stir in asparagus and ½ cup half-and-half. Cover and cook 20 to 30 minutes more or until asparagus is just tender.

Stir in remaining ingredients, then cover and let stand 5 minutes to allow cheese to melt slightly. Fluff with fork and garnish with additional Asiago cheese, if desired, before serving.

TIP: Risotto is a classic creamy rice dish of northern Italy. It can be made with a wide variety of ingredients; fresh vegetables and cheeses such as Asiago work especially well in risottos. Parmesan cheese, shellfish, white wine and herbs are also popular additions.

garlic & herb polenta

SERVINGS: 6 | PREP TIME: 10 MINUTES
HIGH: 3 HOURS | LOW: 4 HOURS

3 tablespoons butter, divided

8 cups water

2 cups yellow corn meal

2 teaspoons finely minced garlic

2 teaspoons salt

3 tablespoons chopped fresh
   herbs such as parsley,
   chives, thyme or chervil (or
   a combination of any of
   these)

Butter inside of 4½- to 5-quart **CROCK-POT®** slow cooker with 1 tablespoon butter. Add water, corn meal, garlic, salt and remaining 2 tablespoons butter; stir. Cover and cook on LOW 4 hours or on HIGH 3 hours, stirring occasionally. Stir in chopped herbs just before serving.

TIP: Polenta may also be poured into a greased pan and allowed to cool until set. Cut into squares (or slice as desired) to serve. For even more great flavor, chill polenta slices until firm then grill or fry until golden brown.

cheesy corn & peppers

SERVINGS: 8 | PREP TIME: 8 MINUTES
HIGH: 2 TO 2½ HOURS

2 pounds frozen corn

2 tablespoons butter, cut into cubes

2 poblano chile peppers, chopped or 1 large green bell pepper and 1 jalapeño, seeded and finely chopped*

½ teaspoon ground cumin

1 teaspoon salt

¼ teaspoon coarsely ground black pepper

3 ounces cream cheese, cut into cubes

1 cup (about 4 ounces) shredded sharp Cheddar cheese

*Poblano and Jalapeño peppers can sting and irritate the skin; wear rubber gloves when handling peppers and do not touch eyes. Wash hands after handling.

Coat inside of 3½- to 4-quart **CROCK-POT®** slow cooker with nonstick cooking spray. Combine all ingredients except cream cheese and Cheddar cheese in **CROCK-POT®** slow cooker. Cover. Cook on HIGH 2 hours.

Stir in cheeses. Cover and cook on HIGH 15 minutes more or until cheeses melt.

chorizo & corn dressing

SERVINGS: 4 TO 6 | PREP TIME: 15 MINUTES
HIGH: 3½ HOURS | LOW: 7 HOURS

½   pound chorizo sausage, removed from casings

1   can (10¾ ounces) condensed cream of chicken soup

1   can (14 ounces) reduced sodium chicken broth

1   box (6 ounces) cornbread stuffing mix

1   cup chopped onions

1   cup diced, seeded red bell pepper

1   cup chopped celery

3   large eggs, lightly beaten

1   cup frozen corn

Lightly spray inside of 3½- to 4-quart **CROCK-POT®** slow cooker with nonstick cooking spray.

Cook chorizo in large skillet over medium-high heat until browned, stirring frequently to break up meat. Transfer to **CROCK-POT®** slow cooker with slotted spoon and return skillet to heat.

Whisk cream of chicken soup and chicken broth into drippings in skillet. Add remaining ingredients and stir until well blended. Stir into **CROCK-POT®** slow cooker. Cover and cook on LOW 7 hours or on HIGH 3½ hours.

cornbread stuffing with sausage & green apples

SERVINGS: 8 TO 12 | PREP TIME: 20 MINUTES

HIGH: 3 TO 3½ HOURS

1	package (16 ounces) honey cornbread mix, plus ingredients to prepare mix*
2	cups cubed French bread
1½	pounds mild Italian sausage, casings removed
1	onion, finely chopped
1	green apple, peeled, cored and diced
2	stalks celery, finely chopped
¼	teaspoon dried sage
¼	teaspoon dried rosemary
¼	teaspoon dried thyme
½	teaspoon salt
¼	teaspoon black pepper
3	cups chicken broth
2	tablespoons chopped fresh parsley (optional)

Or purchase prepared 8-inch square pan of cornbread. Proceed as directed.

Prepare cornbread according to package directions. Cool; cover with plastic wrap and set aside overnight.

Preheat oven to 350°F. Cut cornbread into 1-inch cubes. Spread cornbread and French bread on baking sheet. Toast in oven about 20 minutes or until dry.

Meanwhile, coat inside of 5- to 6-quart **CROCK-POT®** slow cooker with nonstick cooking spray. Cook sausage in medium skillet over medium heat until browned, stirring frequently to break up meat. Transfer sausage to **CROCK-POT®** slow cooker with slotted spoon and return skillet to heat.

Add onion, apple, and celery to skillet. Cook and stir 5 minutes or until onion and apple soften. Stir in sage, rosemary, thyme, salt and pepper. Add to **CROCK-POT®** slow cooker with sausage.

Stir in bread cubes and stir gently to combine. Pour broth over mixture. Cover; cook on HIGH 3 to 3½ hours or until liquid is absorbed. Garnish with parsley.

no-fuss macaroni & cheese

SERVINGS: 6 TO 8 | PREP TIME: 10 MINUTES
LOW: 2 TO 3 HOURS

2   cups (about 8 ounces) uncooked elbow macaroni

4   ounces light pasteurized processed cheese, cubed

1   cup (4 ounces) shredded mild Cheddar cheese

½   teaspoon salt

⅛   teaspoon black pepper

1½ cups fat-free (skim) milk

Combine macaroni, cheeses, salt and pepper in 4½-quart **CROCK-POT®** slow cooker. Pour milk over top. Cover; cook on LOW 2 to 3 hours, stirring after 20 to 30 minutes.

Variation: Stir in sliced hot dogs or desired vegetable.

Note: This is a simple way to make macaroni and cheese without taking the time to boil water and cook noodles. Kids can even make this one on their own.

TIP: As with all macaroni and cheese dishes, as it sits, the cheese sauce thickens and begins to dry out. If it dries out, stir in a little extra milk and heat through. Do not cook longer than 4 hours.

lemon dilled parsnips & turnips

SERVINGS: 8 TO 10 | PREP TIME: 15 MINUTES
HIGH: 1 TO 3 HOURS | LOW: 3 TO 4 HOURS

2   cups chicken broth

¼   cup chopped green onions

4   tablespoons lemon juice

4   tablespoons dried dill

1   teaspoon minced garlic

4   turnips, peeled and cut into ½-inch pieces

3   parsnips, peeled and cut into ½-inch pieces

4   tablespoons cornstarch

¼   cup cold water

Combine broth, green onions, lemon juice, dill and garlic in 4-quart **CROCK-POT®** slow cooker.

Add turnips and parsnips; stir. Cover; cook on LOW 3 to 4 hours or on HIGH 1 to 3 hours.

Turn CROCK-POT® slow cooker to HIGH. Stir cornstarch into water in small bowl. Add to **CROCK-POT®** slow cooker. Stir well to combine. Cover; continue cooking 15 minutes longer or until thickened.

lemon & tangerine glazed carrots

SERVINGS: 10 TO 12 | PREP TIME: 15 MINUTES
HIGH: 1 TO 3 HOURS | LOW: 4 TO 5 HOURS

6 cups sliced carrots

1½ cups apple juice

6 tablespoons butter

¼ cup packed brown sugar

2 tablespoons grated lemon peel

2 tablespoons grated tangerine peel

½ teaspoon salt

Chopped fresh parsley (optional)

Combine all ingredients except parsley in 4-quart **CROCK-POT®** slow cooker. Cover; cook on LOW 4 to 5 hours or on HIGH 1 to 3 hours. Garnish with chopped parsley.

lentils with walnuts

SERVINGS: 4 TO 6 | PREP TIME: 10 MINUTES
HIGH: 3 HOURS

1   cup brown lentils

1   very small onion or large shallot, chopped

1   celery stalk, trimmed and chopped

1   large carrot, chopped

¼   teaspoon crushed dried thyme

3   cups chicken broth

    Salt and black pepper

¼   cup chopped walnuts

Combine lentils, onion, celery, carrot, thyme and broth in 4-quart **CROCK-POT®** slow cooker. Cover; cook on HIGH 3 hours. Do not overcook. (Lentils should absorb most or all of broth. Slightly tilt slow cooker to check.)

Season with salt and pepper. Spoon lentils into serving bowl and sprinkle with walnuts.

Variation: If desired, top with 4 slices cooked bacon, crumbled or cut into bite-size pieces. To serve as a main dish, stir in 1 cup diced cooked ham.

potato casserole with creamy cheese sauce

SERVINGS: 8 | PREP TIME: 30 MINUTES

HIGH: 3 HOURS

2	pounds russet potatoes, sliced
2	medium yellow squash, cut into ¼-inch slices
1	cup chopped onions
1	cup diced, seeded red bell pepper
⅓	cup water
2	tablespoons butter
¾	teaspoon dried thyme leaves
¾	teaspoon salt
¼	teaspoon ground black pepper
⅛	teaspoon ground red pepper
½	cup half-and-half
8	slices American cheese

Place all ingredients except half-and-half and cheese into 4½-quart **CROCK-POT®** slow cooker in order listed above. Cover; cook on HIGH 3 hours.

Remove vegetables with slotted spoon; place in serving bowl. Stir half-and-half and cheese into **CROCK-POT®** slow cooker. Cover; cook 5 minutes or until cheese melts. Whisk until well blended; pour over vegetables.

jim's mexican-style spinach

SERVINGS: 6 | PREP TIME: 45 MINUTES
LOW: 4 TO 6 HOURS

3   packages (10 ounces each) frozen chopped spinach

1   onion, chopped

1   clove garlic, minced

1   tablespoon canola oil

2   Anaheim chiles, toasted, peeled and minced*

3   fresh tomatillos, toasted, husks removed and chopped**

6   tablespoons fat-free sour cream (optional)

Chiles can sting and irritate the skin, so wear rubber gloves when handling peppers and do not touch your eyes.

**To toast fresh tomatillos, preheat heavy frying pan over medium heat. Leaving papery husks on, toast tomatillos, turning often, about 10 minutes or until husks are brown and interior flesh is soft. Remove from heat. When cool enough to handle, remove and discard husks.*

Place frozen spinach in 4½-quart **CROCK-POT®** slow cooker.

Cook and stir onion and garlic in oil in large skillet over medium heat about 5 minutes or until onion is softened. Add chiles and tomatillos; cook and stir 2 to 3 minutes. Transfer mixture to **CROCK-POT®** slow cooker. Cover; cook on LOW 4 to 6 hours. Stir before serving. Top with dollops of sour cream, if desired.

Substitution: Two pounds of fresh spinach (about 5 quarts) or other greens such as bagged baby spinach or mixed wild greens can be substituted for the frozen spinach. If using fresh bundled spinach, be sure to trim the stems and thoroughly wash the leaves in several changes of water to remove any sand before chopping.

TIP: To toast chiles, heat a griddle or cast-iron skillet over medium-high heat until a drop of water sizzles. Cook chiles, a few at a time, turning occasionally with tongs, until they are blackened all over. (Chiles can also be held directly in a gas flame with a long-handled fork.)

mrs. grady's beans

SERVINGS: 6 TO 8 | PREP TIME: 15 MINUTES
LOW: 2 TO 3 HOURS

½   pound 90% lean ground beef

1   small onion, chopped

8   slices bacon, chopped

1   can (about 15 ounces) pinto beans, undrained

1   can (about 15 ounces) butter beans, rinsed and drained, reserving ¼ cup liquid

1   can (about 15 ounces) kidney beans, rinsed and drained

¼   cup ketchup

2   tablespoons molasses

½   teaspoon dry mustard

½   cup granulated sugar

¼   cup packed brown sugar

Brown ground beef, onion and bacon in medium saucepan over high heat. Stir in beans and liquid; set aside.

Combine ketchup, molasses and mustard in medium bowl. Mix in sugars. Stir ketchup mixture into beef mixture; mix well. Transfer to 4½-quart **CROCK-POT®** slow cooker. Cover and cook on LOW 2 to 3 hours or until heated through.

mexican-style rice & cheese

SERVINGS: 6 TO 8 | PREP TIME: 10 MINUTES
LOW: 6 TO 8 HOURS

1   can (about 15 ounces) Mexican-style beans, rinsed and drained

1   can (about 14 ounces) diced tomatoes with jalapeños, undrained*

2   cups (8 ounces) shredded Monterey Jack or Colby cheese, divided

1½   cups uncooked converted long-grain rice

1   large onion, finely chopped

½   (8-ounce) package cream cheese

3   cloves garlic, minced

Jalapeños can sting and irritate the skin, so wear rubber gloves when handling peppers and do not touch your eyes.

Spray inside of 4½-quart **CROCK-POT**® slow cooker with nonstick cooking spray. Combine beans, tomatoes, 1 cup cheese, rice, onion, cream cheese and garlic in **CROCK-POT**® slow cooker; mix well.

Cover; cook on LOW 6 to 8 hours or until rice is tender but not overcooked.

Sprinkle with remaining 1 cup cheese just before serving.

artichoke & tomato paella

SERVINGS: 8 | PREP TIME: 35 MINUTES
HIGH: 2 HOURS | LOW: 4 HOURS

4   cups vegetable broth

2   cups converted white rice

½   (10-ounce) package frozen chopped spinach, thawed and drained

1   green bell pepper, seeded and chopped

1   medium ripe tomato, sliced into wedges

1   medium yellow onion, chopped

1   medium carrot, peeled and diced

3   cloves garlic, minced

1   tablespoon minced flat-leaf parsley

1   teaspoon salt

½   teaspoon black pepper

1   can (13¾ ounces) artichoke hearts, quartered, rinsed and well-drained

½   cup frozen peas

Combine broth, rice, spinach, bell pepper, tomato, onion, carrot, garlic, parsley, salt and pepper in 4½-quart **CROCK-POT®** slow cooker. Mix thoroughly. Cover; cook on LOW 4 hours or on HIGH 2 hours.

Before serving, add artichoke hearts and peas. Cover; cook on HIGH 15 minutes. Mix well before serving.

TIP: Paella is a classic Spanish rice dish. It traditionally includes a variety of shellfish and meat, onions, garlic, tomatoes and often peas, but is also wonderful just with simple vegetables. There is no standard recipe; paella varies from region to region and from cook to cook.

braised sweet & sour cabbage & apples

SERVINGS: 4 TO 6 | PREP TIME: 15 MINUTES
LOW: 2½ TO 3 HOURS

2   tablespoons unsalted butter

6   cups coarsely shredded red cabbage

1   large sweet apple, peeled, cored and cut into bite-size pieces

3   whole cloves

½   cup raisins

½   cup apple cider

3   tablespoons cider vinegar, divided

2   tablespoons packed dark brown sugar

½   teaspoon salt

¼   teaspoon black pepper

Melt butter in very large skillet or shallow pot over medium heat. Add cabbage. Cook and stir 3 minutes or until cabbage is glossy. Transfer to 5-quart **CROCK-POT**® slow cooker.

Add apple, cloves, raisins, apple cider, 2 tablespoons vinegar, brown sugar, salt and pepper. Cover; cook on LOW 2½ to 3 hours.

To serve, remove cloves and stir in remaining 1 tablespoon vinegar.

busy-day rice

2   cups water

1   cup uncooked converted white
     rice

2   tablespoons butter

1   tablespoon dried minced onion

1   tablespoon dried parsley

2   teaspoons chicken bouillon
     granules

     Dash ground red pepper
     (optional)

Combine all ingredients in 4½-quart **CROCK-POT®** slow cooker; mix well. Cover; cook on HIGH 2 hours.

Variation: During the last 30 minutes of cooking, add ½ cup green peas, tiny broccoli florets or diced carrots.

creamy red pepper polenta

SERVINGS: 4 TO 6 | PREP TIME: 10 MINUTES
HIGH: 1 OR 2 HOURS | LOW: 3 TO 4 HOURS

¼ cup (½ stick) butter, melted

¼ teaspoon paprika, plus
    additional for garnish

⅛ teaspoon ground red pepper

⅛ teaspoon ground cumin

6 cups boiling water

2 cups yellow cornmeal

1 small red bell pepper, cored,
    seeded and finely chopped

2 teaspoons salt

Combine butter, paprika, red pepper and cumin in 4½-quart **CROCK-POT®** slow cooker. Add hot water, cornmeal, red pepper and salt. Stir well to combine. Cover; cook on LOW 3 to 4 hours or on HIGH 1 to 2 hours, stirring occasionally. Garnish with additional paprika, if desired.

oriental golden barley with cashews

SERVINGS: 4 | PREP TIME: 20 MINUTES
HIGH: 2 TO 3 HOURS | LOW: 4 TO 5 HOURS

2	tablespoons unsalted butter
1	cup hulled barley, sorted
3	cups vegetable broth
1	cup chopped celery
1	green bell pepper, cored, seeded and chopped
1	yellow onion, peeled and minced
1	clove garlic, minced
¼	teaspoon black pepper
¼	cup finely chopped cashews

Heat skillet over medium heat until hot. Add butter and barley. Cook and stir about 10 minutes or until barley is slightly browned. Transfer to 4-quart **CROCK-POT®** slow cooker.

Add broth, celery, bell pepper, onion, garlic and black pepper. Stir well to combine. Cover; cook on LOW 4 to 5 hours or on HIGH 2 to 3 hours or until barley is tender and liquid is absorbed.

To serve, garnish with cashews.

TIP: Barley is rich in both soluble and insoluble fiber. A recent study suggests that barley may also have a cholesterol-lowering effect similar to oat bran.

wild rice with fruit & nuts

SERVINGS: 6 TO 8 | PREP TIME: 10 MINUTES
HIGH: 2½ TO 3 HOURS | LOW: 7 HOURS

2   cups wild rice (or wild rice blend), rinsed*

½   cup dried cranberries

½   cup chopped raisins

½   cup chopped dried apricots

½   cup almond slivers, toasted**

5   to 6 cups chicken broth

1   cup orange juice

2   tablespoons butter, melted

1   teaspoon ground cumin

2   green onions, thinly sliced

2   to 3 tablespoons chopped fresh parsley

Salt and black pepper, to taste

*Do not use parboiled rice or a blend containing parboiled rice.
**To toast almonds, spread in single layer in heavy-bottomed skillet. Cook over medium heat 1 to 2 minutes, stirring frequently, until nuts are lightly browned. Remove from skillet immediately. Cool before using.

Combine wild rice, cranberries, raisins, apricots and almonds in 4½-quart **CROCK-POT®** slow cooker. Combine broth, orange juice, butter and cumin in medium bowl. Pour mixture over rice and stir to mix.

Cover; cook on LOW 7 hours or on HIGH 2½ to 3 hours. Stir once, adding more hot broth if necessary. When rice is soft, add green onions and parsley. Adjust seasonings, if desired. Cook 10 minutes longer and serve.

Bracing
Beverages

mucho mocha cocoa

SERVINGS: 9 CUPS | PREP TIME: 5 MINUTES

LOW: 3 HOURS

1	cup chocolate syrup
⅓	cup instant coffee granules
2	tablespoons sugar (or more to taste)
2	whole cinnamon sticks
1	quart whole milk
1	quart half-and-half

Combine all ingredients in 3½- to 4-quart **CROCK-POT®** slow cooker. Stir until well blended. Cover and cook on LOW 3 hours. Serve hot in mugs.

TIP: This is great for a party. If desired, add 1 ounce of rum or whisky to each serving.

spiced citrus tea

SERVINGS: ABOUT 4 | PREP TIME: 15 MINUTES
LOW: 3 HOURS

4   tea bags

    Peel of 1 orange

4   cups boiling water

2   cans (6 ounces each) orange-
    pineapple juice

3   tablespoons honey

3   star anise

3   cinnamon sticks

    Fresh strawberries, raspberries
    or kiwi (optional)

Place tea bags and orange peel in 4½-quart **CROCK-POT®** slow cooker. Pour in boiling water. Cover and let steep 10 minutes. Discard tea bags and orange peel.

Add remaining ingredients except fresh fruit. Cover; cook on LOW 3 hours.

Garnish with strawberries, raspberries or kiwi wedges.

mulled cranberry tea

SERVINGS: 8 | PREP TIME: 10 MINUTES
HIGH: 1 TO 2 HOURS | LOW: 2 TO 3 HOURS

2 tea bags

1 cup boiling water

1 bottle (48 ounces) cranberry juice

½ cup dried cranberries (optional)

⅓ cup sugar

1 large lemon, cut into ¼-inch slices

4 cinnamon sticks

6 whole cloves

Additional thin lemon slices and cinnamon sticks (optional)

Place tea bags in 4½-quart **CROCK-POT®** slow cooker. Pour boiling water over tea bags; cover and let stand 5 minutes. Remove and discard tea bags. Stir in cranberry juice, cranberries, if desired, sugar, lemon slices, 4 cinnamon sticks and cloves. Cover; cook on LOW 2 to 3 hours or on HIGH 1 to 2 hours.

Remove and discard lemon slices, cinnamon sticks and cloves. Serve in warm mugs garnished with additional lemon slices and cinnamon sticks, if desired.

TIP: This kid-friendly version of mulled wine is sure to be a hit with family or guests. The festive flavors will spice up any afternoon, meal or after-dinner treat. The cranberries and spices go well with holiday foods, but this drink can be enjoyed all year.

chai tea

SERVINGS: 8 TO 10 | PREP TIME: 8 MINUTES
HIGH: 2 TO 2½ HOURS

2 quarts (8 cups) water

8 bags black tea

¾ cup sugar*

16 whole cloves

16 whole cardamom seeds, pods removed (optional)

5 cinnamon sticks

8 slices fresh ginger

1 cup milk

*Chai Tea is typically a sweet drink. For less sweet tea, reduce sugar to ½ cup.

Combine all ingredients except milk in 4½-quart **CROCK-POT®** slow cooker. Cover; cook on HIGH 2 to 2½ hours.

Strain mixture; discard solids. Tea may be covered and refrigerated (for up to 3 days) at this point.

Stir in milk just before serving. Serve warm or chilled.

ginger-lime martini

SERVINGS: 8 | PREP TIME: 10 MINUTES
HIGH: 3 TO 4 HOURS | LOW: 6 TO 8 HOURS

2 cups sugar

1 cup water

1 (5-inch) piece fresh ginger, peeled and thinly sliced

3 cups vodka, chilled

2 cups lime juice

Crushed ice

Place sugar, water and ginger into 4½-quart **CROCK-POT®** slow cooker. Cover and cook on HIGH 3 to 4 hours or on LOW 6 to 8 hours.

Strain and cool. Refrigerate in airtight container (up to 7 days) until needed.

To serve combine 2 ounces ginger syrup, 3 ounces vodka and 2 ounces lime juice in martini shaker half filled with crushed ice. Shake to combine and then strain into chilled martini glass. Repeat with remaining ingredients.

Variation: Homemade Ginger Ale: Pour ½ cup chilled ginger syrup over ice in 16-ounce glass; top off with 1 cup soda water and stir gently to combine.

chai tea

hot mulled cider

SERVINGS: 16 | PREP TIME: 5 MINUTES
LOW: 5 TO 6 HOURS

½ gallon apple cider

½ cup packed light brown sugar

1½ teaspoons balsamic or cider vinegar (optional)

1 teaspoon vanilla

1 cinnamon stick

6 whole cloves

½ cup applejack or bourbon (optional)

Combine all ingredients except applejack in 4½-quart **CROCK-POT®** slow cooker. Cover; cook on LOW 5 to 6 hours. Remove and discard cinnamon stick and cloves. Stir in applejack just before serving, if desired. Serve hot in mugs.

infused mint mojito

SERVINGS: 10 TO 12 | PREP TIME: 10 MINUTES
HIGH: 3½ HOURS

2 cups water

2 cups sugar

2 bunches fresh mint, stems removed

¾ to 1 cup fresh-squeezed lime juice

1 bottle (750 ml) light rum

2 liters club soda

Fresh mint to garnish

Place water, sugar and mint in 4½-quart **CROCK-POT®** slow cooker. Cover and cook on HIGH 3½ hours.

Strain into large pitcher. Stir in lime juice and rum. Cover and refrigerate until cold.

To serve, fill tall glasses halfway with fresh ice. Pour ¾ cup mint syrup over ice; top off with club soda to taste. Garnish with additional fresh mint leaves and serve immediately.

hot mulled cider

viennese coffee

SERVINGS: ABOUT 4 | PREP TIME: 5 MINUTES
LOW: 2½ TO 3 HOURS

3	cups strong freshly brewed hot coffee
3	tablespoons chocolate syrup
1	teaspoon sugar
⅓	cup whipping cream
¼	cup crème de cacao or Irish cream (optional)
	Whipped cream (optional)
	Chocolate shavings (optional)

Combine coffee, chocolate syrup and sugar in 4½-quart **CROCK-POT®** slow cooker. Cover and cook on LOW 2 to 2½ hours. Stir in whipping cream and crème de cacao, if desired. Cover and cook 30 minutes or until heated through.

Ladle coffee into coffee cups. Top with whipped cream and chocolate shavings.

cinnamon latté

SERVINGS: 6 TO 8 | PREP TIME: 5 MINUTES
HIGH: 3 HOURS

6	cups double-strength brewed coffee*
2	cups half-and-half
1	cup sugar
1	teaspoon vanilla
3	cinnamon sticks, plus additional for garnish
	Whipped cream (optional)

Double the amount of coffee grounds normally used to brew coffee. Or substitute 8 teaspoons instant coffee dissolved in 6 cups boiling water.

Blend coffee, half-and-half, sugar and vanilla in 4½-quart **CROCK-POT®** slow cooker. Add 3 cinnamon sticks. Cover; cook on HIGH 3 hours.

Remove cinnamon sticks. Serve latté in tall coffee mugs with dollop of whipped cream and cinnamon stick, if desired.

viennese coffee

hot tropics sipper

SERVINGS: 8 | PREP TIME: 5 MINUTES
HIGH: 3½ TO 4 HOURS

4   cups pineapple juice

2   cups apple juice

1   container (11.3 ounces) apricot
    nectar

3   whole cinnamon sticks

6   whole cloves

½   cup packed dark brown sugar

1   medium lemon, thinly sliced

1   medium orange, thinly sliced

    Additional orange and lemon
    slices (optional)

Place all ingredients in 4½-quart **CROCK-POT**® slow cooker. Cover; cook on HIGH 3½ to 4 hours or until very fragrant. Strain immediately (beverage will turn bitter if fruit and spices remain after cooking is complete). Garnish with fresh orange and lemon slices, if desired.

triple delicious hot chocolate

SERVINGS: 6 | PREP TIME: 30 MINUTES
LOW: 2 HOURS

3   cups milk, divided

⅓   cup sugar

¼   cup unsweetened cocoa
     powder

¼   teaspoon salt

¾   teaspoon vanilla

1   cup whipping cream

1   square (1 ounce) white
     chocolate, chopped

1   square (1 ounce) bittersweet
     chocolate, chopped

¾   cup whipped cream

3   teaspoons mini chocolate
     chips or shaved bittersweet
     chocolate

Combine ½ cup milk, sugar, cocoa and salt in medium bowl; beat until smooth. Pour into 4½-quart **CROCK-POT®** slow cooker. Add remaining 2½ cups milk and vanilla. Cover; cook on LOW 2 hours.

Add cream. Cover and cook on LOW 10 minutes. Stir in white and bittersweet chocolates until melted.

Pour hot chocolate into 6 coffee cups. Top each with 2 tablespoons whipped cream and ½ teaspoon chocolate chips.

mulled wine

SERVINGS: 12 | PREP TIME: 10 MINUTES
HIGH: 2 TO 2½ HOURS

2   bottles (750 ml each) dry red wine, such as Cabernet Sauvignon
1   cup light corn syrup
1   cup water
1   square (8 inches) double-thickness cheesecloth
    Peel of 1 large orange
1   cinnamon stick, broken in half
8   whole cloves
1   whole nutmeg

Combine wine, corn syrup and water in 4½-quart **CROCK-POT®** slow cooker.

Rinse cheesecloth; squeeze out water. Wrap orange peel, cinnamon stick, cloves and nutmeg in cheesecloth. Tie bag securely with cotton string or strip of cheesecloth. Add to **CROCK-POT®** slow cooker. Cover; cook on HIGH 2 to 2½ hours.

Remove spice bag and discard. Ladle wine into mugs. Garnish as desired.

TIP: Mulled wine is a wonderful and warming beverage to serve at a holiday party. The spices will fill the kitchen with festive aromas, and the sweet and fruity flavors pair well with rich holiday food and desserts.

warm & spicy fruit punch

SERVINGS: 14 | PREP TIME: 10 MINUTES

LOW: 5 TO 6 HOURS

4   cinnamon sticks

1   orange

1   teaspoon whole allspice

½   teaspoon whole cloves

7   cups water

1   can (12 ounces) frozen
    cranberry-raspberry juice
    concentrate, thawed

1   can (6 ounces) frozen lemonade
    concentrate, thawed

2   cans (5½ ounces each) apricot
    nectar

Break cinnamon sticks into pieces. Using vegetable peeler, remove strips of orange peel. Squeeze juice from orange; set aside. Bundle cinnamon sticks, orange peel, allspice and cloves in cheesecloth and tie securely.

Combine orange juice, water, juice concentrates and apricot nectar in 4-quart **CROCK-POT®** slow cooker; add spice bag. Cover; cook on LOW 5 to 6 hours.

Remove and discard spice bundle.

spiced apple tea

SERVINGS: 4 | PREP TIME: 5 MINUTES

LOW: 2 TO 3 HOURS

3   bags cinnamon herbal tea

3   cups boiling water

2   cups unsweetened apple juice

6   whole cloves

1   cinnamon stick

Place tea bags in 4½-quart **CROCK-POT®** slow cooker. Pour boiling water over tea bags; cover and let stand 10 minutes. Remove and discard tea bags. Add apple juice, cloves and cinnamon stick to **CROCK-POT®** slow cooker. Cover; cook on LOW 2 to 3 hours. Remove and discard cloves and cinnamon stick. Serve warm in mugs.

The Sweet Table

glazed orange poppy seed cake

SERVINGS: 8 | PREP TIME: 20 MINUTES
HIGH: 1½ HOURS TO 1¾ HOURS

BATTER

1½	cups biscuit baking mix
¾	cup granulated sugar
2	tablespoons poppy seeds
½	cup sour cream
1	egg
2	tablespoons milk
1	teaspoon vanilla
2	teaspoons orange zest

GLAZE

¼	cup orange juice
2	cups powdered sugar, sifted
2	teaspoons poppy seeds

Coat inside of 4-quart **CROCK-POT®** slow cooker with nonstick cooking spray. Cut waxed paper circle to fit bottom of **CROCK-POT®** slow cooker (trace insert bottom and cut slightly smaller to fit). Spray lightly with cooking spray.

Whisk together baking mix, sugar and poppy seeds in medium bowl; set aside. In another bowl, blend sour cream, egg, milk, vanilla and orange zest. Whisk wet ingredients into dry mixture until thoroughly blended.

Spoon batter into prepared **CROCK-POT®** slow cooker and smooth top. Place paper towel under lid, then cover. Cook on HIGH 1 hour 30 minutes. (Cake is done when top is no longer shiny and a toothpick inserted in center comes out clean.)

Invert cake onto cooling rack, peel off waxed paper and allow to cool (right-side-up) on cooling rack.

Whisk orange juice into powdered sugar. Cut cake into 8 wedges and place on cooling rack with a tray underneath to catch drips. With a small spatula or knife, spread glaze over top and cut sides of each wedge. Sprinkle poppy seeds over wedges and allow glaze to set.

tequila-poached pears

SERVINGS: 4 | PREP TIME: 15 MINUTES
HIGH: 2 TO 3 HOURS | LOW: 4 TO 6 HOURS

4   Anjou pears, peeled

1   cup tequila

¾   cup sugar

    Juice and zest of 1 lime, plus extra for garnish

1   can (11½ ounces) pear nectar

2   cups water

Place pears in 4½-quart **CROCK-POT®** slow cooker.

Add remaining ingredients to medium saucepan. Stir over medium high heat until mixture boils. Boil 1 minute and pour over pears. Cover and cook on LOW 4 to 6 hours or on HIGH 2 to 3 hours or until pears are tender.

Serve warm with vanilla ice cream, or chill and serve on chilled plate drizzled with poaching liquid and sprinkled with lime zest.

TIP: Poaching fruit in a sugar, wine, juice or alcohol syrup helps the fruit retain its shape and adds flavor.

figs poached in red wine

SERVINGS: 4 | PREP TIME: 5 MINUTES
HIGH: 4 TO 5 HOURS | LOW: 5 TO 6 HOURS

2   cups dry red wine

1   cup packed brown sugar

2   (3-inch) cinnamon sticks

1   teaspoon finely grated orange
    zest

12 dried calimyrna or
    Mediterranean figs (about 6
    ounces)

4   tablespoons heavy cream
    (optional)

Stir together wine, brown sugar, cinnamon sticks, orange zest and figs in 2- to 4½-quart **CROCK-POT®** slow cooker. Cover and cook on LOW for 5 to 6 hours or on HIGH 4 to 5 hours.

To serve, spoon some figs and syrup into serving dish. Top with spoonful of cream. May be served warm or cold.

the claus's christmas pudding

SERVINGS: 12 | PREP TIME: 30 TO 35 MINUTES
LOW: 5½ HOURS

PUDDING

- ⅔ cups sweetened dried cranberries
- ⅔ cup golden raisins
- ½ cup whole candied red cherries, halved
- ¾ cup plus 2 tablespoons cream sherry, divided
- 18 slices cranberry or other fruited bread
- 3 egg yolks, beaten
- 1½ cups light cream
- ⅓ cup granulated sugar
- ¼ teaspoon kosher salt
- 1½ teaspoons cherry extract
- 1 cup white chocolate chips
- 1 cup hot water

SAUCE

- 2 egg yolks, beaten
- ¼ cup powdered sugar, sifted
- ¼ teaspoon vanilla
- ½ cup whipping cream

Preheat oven to 250°F. Generously butter 6½-cup ceramic or glass bowl. Place cranberries and raisins in small bowl; set aside. Place cherries in another bowl. Heat ¾ cup sherry until warm, and pour over cherries; set aside.

Place bread slices on baking sheet and bake 5 minutes. Turn over and bake 5 minutes or until bread is dry. Cool, then cut into ½-inch cubes.

Combine 3 egg yolks, light cream, granulated sugar and salt in heavy saucepan. Cook and stir over medium heat until mixture coats metal spoon. Remove from heat. Set saucepan in sink of ice water to cool quickly; stir 1 to 2 minutes. Stir in cherry extract. Transfer cooled mixture to large bowl. Fold bread cubes into custard until coated.

Drain cherries, reserving sherry. Arrange one-fourth of cherries, plus ⅓ cup raisin mixture and ¼ cup white chocolate chips in prepared ceramic bowl. Add one-fourth of bread cube mixture. Sprinkle with reserved sherry drained from cherries. Repeat layers 3 times, arranging fruit near edges of bowl. Pour remaining reserved sherry over all.

Cover bowl tightly with foil. Place in 4-quart **CROCK-POT®** slow cooker. Pour hot water around bowl. Cover; cook on LOW 5½ hours. Remove bowl and let stand on wire rack 10 to 15 minutes before unmolding.

TO PREPARE SAUCE: Combine 2 egg yolks, powdered sugar, remaining 2 tablespoons sherry and vanilla. Beat whipping cream in small bowl until small peaks form. Fold whipped cream into egg yolk mixture. Cover; chill until serving time. Serve with warm pudding.

pecan-cinnamon pudding cake

SERVINGS: 8 | PREP TIME: 20 MINUTES
HIGH: 1¼ TO 1½ HOURS

1⅓   cups all-purpose flour
½   cup granulated sugar
1½   teaspoons baking powder
1½   teaspoons ground cinnamon
⅔   cup milk
5   tablespoons butter or
       margarine, melted, divided
1   cup chopped pecans
1½   cups water
¾   cup packed brown sugar
     Whipped cream (optional)

Stir together flour, granulated sugar, baking powder and cinnamon in medium bowl. Add milk and 3 tablespoons butter; mix just until blended. Stir in pecans. Spread in bottom of 4-quart **CROCK-POT®** slow cooker.

Combine water, brown sugar and remaining 2 tablespoons butter in small saucepan; bring to a boil. Pour over batter in **CROCK-POT®** slow cooker.

Cover; cook on HIGH 1¼ to 1½ hours or until toothpick inserted into center comes out clean. Let stand, uncovered, 30 minutes. Serve warm with whipped cream.

TIP: Chopping nuts such as pecans can often result in nuts flying across the kitchen. Warm the nuts to make chopping easier: place 1 cup of shelled nuts in a microwavable dish and heat on HIGH about 30 seconds or just until warm; chop as desired.

peanut fudge pudding cake

SERVINGS: 4 | PREP TIME: 15 MINUTES
HIGH: 1¼ TO 1½ HOURS

1	cup all-purpose flour
1	cup sugar, divided
1½	teaspoons baking powder
⅔	cup milk
2	tablespoons vegetable oil
1	teaspoon vanilla
½	cup peanut butter
¼	cup unsweetened cocoa powder
1	cup boiling water
	Chopped peanuts (optional)
	Vanilla ice cream (optional)

Coat 4½-quart **CROCK-POT®** slow cooker with nonstick cooking spray or butter. Combine flour, ½ cup sugar and baking powder in medium bowl. Add milk, oil, vanilla and peanut butter. Mix until well blended. Pour batter into **CROCK-POT®** slow cooker.

Combine remaining ½ cup sugar and cocoa powder in small bowl. Stir in water. Pour into **CROCK-POT®** slow cooker. Do not stir.

Cover; cook on HIGH 1¼ to 1½ hours or until toothpick inserted into center comes out clean. Allow cake to rest 10 minutes, then scoop into serving dishes or invert onto serving platter. Serve warm with chopped peanuts and ice cream, if desired.

TIP: Because this recipe makes its own fudge topping, be sure to spoon some of it from the bottom of the **CROCK-POT®** slow cooker when serving, or invert the cake for a luscious chocolately finish.

bittersweet chocolate-espresso crème brûlée

SERVINGS: 5 | PREP TIME: 10 MINUTES
LOW: 1 TO 2 HOURS

½ cup chopped bittersweet
    chocolate
5 egg yolks
1¾ cups heavy cream
¼ cup espresso
½ cup granulated sugar
¼ cup Demerara or raw sugar

Arrange 5 6-ounce ramekins or custard cups inside 4½-quart **CROCK-POT®** slow cooker. Pour enough water to come halfway up sides of ramekins (taking care to keep water out of ramekins themselves)

Divide chocolate among ramekins.

Whisk egg yolks briefly; set aside. Heat cream, espresso and granulated sugar in small saucepan over medium heat, stirring constantly, until mixture begins to boil. Pour hot cream in thin, steady stream into egg yolks, whisking constantly. Pour through fine mesh strainer into clean bowl.

Ladle into prepared ramekins in bottom of **CROCK-POT®** slow cooker. Cover and cook on HIGH 1 to 2 hours or until custard is set around edges but still soft in centers. Carefully remove and cool to room temperature, then cover and refrigerate until serving.

Spread tops of custards with Demerara sugar just before serving; melt with kitchen torch. Serve immediately.

fruit & nut baked apples

SERVINGS: 4 | PREP TIME: 20 MINUTES
LOW: 3 TO 4 HOURS

4   large baking apples, such as Rome Beauty or Jonathan

1   tablespoon lemon juice

⅓   cup chopped dried apricots

⅓   cup chopped walnuts or pecans

3   tablespoons packed light brown sugar

½   teaspoon ground cinnamon

2   tablespoons melted butter or margarine

    Caramel ice cream topping (optional)

Scoop out center of each apple, leaving 1½-inch-wide cavity about ½ inch from bottom. Peel top of apple down about 1 inch. Brush peeled edges evenly with lemon juice. Mix apricots, walnuts, brown sugar and cinnamon in small bowl. Add butter; mix well. Spoon mixture evenly into apple cavities.

Pour ½ cup water in bottom of 4½-quart **CROCK-POT®** slow cooker. Place 2 apples in bottom of **CROCK-POT®** slow cooker. Arrange remaining 2 apples above but not directly on top of bottom apples.

Cover; cook on LOW 3 to 4 hours or until apples are tender. Serve warm or at room temperature with caramel ice cream topping, if desired.

TIP: Ever wonder why you need to brush lemon juice around the top of an apple? Citrus fruits contain an acid that keeps apples, potatoes and other white vegetables from discoloring once they are cut or peeled.

cran-cherry bread pudding

SERVINGS: 12 | PREP TIME: 20 TO 25 MINUTES

LOW: 3½ TO 5½ HOURS

3   large egg yolks, beaten

1½   cups light cream

⅓   cup sugar

¼   teaspoon kosher salt

1½   teaspoons cherry extract

⅔   cup dried sweetened cranberries

⅔   cup golden raisins

½   cup whole candied red cherries, cut in half

¾   cup sherry

9   cups unseasoned bread stuffing croutons or 18 slices bread, dried in oven and cut into ½-inch cubes

1   cup white chocolate chips

Whipped cream

Combine egg yolks, cream, sugar and salt in medium heavy saucepan. Cook and stir over medium heat until mixture coats metal spoon. Remove custard from heat; cool at once by setting saucepan in sink of ice water and stirring 1 to 2 minutes. Stir in cherry extract. Place custard in large mixing bowl. Cover surface with clear plastic wrap; refrigerate.

Combine cranberries, raisins and cherries in small bowl. Heat sherry until warm. Pour over fruits; let stand 10 minutes.

Fold bread cubes and white chocolate chips into custard, until coated. Drain fruits, reserving sherry. Mix fruits with bread cube mixture. Grease 2-quart baking dish that will fit in 5-, 6- or 7-quart **CROCK-POT®** slow cooker. Pour bread and fruit mixture into prepared dish. Lightly press with back of spoon. Pour reserved sherry over bread mixture; cover dish tightly with foil.

Make foil handles (see note below). Use foil handles to set dish in **CROCK-POT®** slow cooker. Pour water around dish to depth of 1 inch. Cover; cook on LOW 3½ to 5½ hours or until pudding springs back when touched. Carefully remove dish using foil handles; uncover and let stand 10 minutes. Serve warm with whipped cream.

Note: To make foil handles, tear off 3 (18×2-inch) strips of heavy-duty foil or use regular foil folded to double thickness. Crisscross foil strips in spoke design and place dish on center of strips. Pull foil strips up and over dish.

gingerbread

SERVINGS: 6 TO 8 | PREP TIME: 10 TO 15 MINUTES

HIGH: 1½ TO 1¾ HOURS

½	cup (1 stick) butter, softened
½	cup sugar
1	egg, lightly beaten
1	cup light molasses
2½	cups all-purpose flour
1½	teaspoons baking soda
1	teaspoon ground cinnamon
2	teaspoons ground ginger
½	teaspoon ground cloves
½	teaspoon salt
1	cup hot water
	Whipped cream (optional)

Coat 4½-quart **CROCK-POT®** slow cooker with butter or nonstick cooking spray. Beat together butter and sugar in large bowl. Add egg, molasses, flour, baking soda, cinnamon, ginger, cloves and salt. Stir in hot water and mix well. Pour batter into **CROCK-POT®** slow cooker.

Cover; cook on HIGH 1½ to 1¾ hours or until toothpick inserted into center of cake comes out clean. Serve warm; top with whipped cream.

TIP: Spice up your mornings and turn this flavorful cake into breakfast. Gingerbread is a tasty breakfast treat when served with a mild cheese like Danish Havarti, Jarlsberg or baby Swiss.

chocolate hazelnut pudding cake

SERVINGS: 10 | PREP TIME: 5 MINUTES
HIGH: 2½ HOURS

1	box (18¼ ounces) golden yellow cake mix
1	cup water
4	eggs
½	cup sour cream
½	cup vegetable oil
1	cup semisweet mini chocolate chips
½	cup chopped hazelnuts
	Whipped cream or ice cream (optional)

Coat 6-quart **CROCK-POT**® slow cooker with nonstick cooking spray. Combine cake mix, water, eggs, sour cream and oil; mix until smooth. Pour batter into **CROCK-POT**® slow cooker. Cover; cook on HIGH 2 hours or until batter is nearly set.

Sprinkle on mini chocolate chips and hazelnuts. Cover; cook 30 minutes longer or until toothpick inserted into center comes out clean or cake begins to pull away from sides of **CROCK-POT**® slow cooker. Let stand until cool and slice or spoon out while warm. Serve with whipped cream or ice cream, if desired.

chocolate chip lemon cake

SERVINGS: 8 | PREP TIME: 15 MINUTES
HIGH: 1¾ TO 2 HOURS | LOW: 3 TO 4 HOURS

¾ cup granulated sugar

½ cup shortening

2 eggs, lightly beaten

1⅔ cups all-purpose flour

1½ teaspoons baking powder

¼ teaspoon salt

¾ cup milk

½ cup chocolate chips

Grated peel of 1 lemon

Juice of 1 lemon

¼ to ½ cup powdered sugar

Melted chocolate (optional)

Turn 4½-quart **CROCK-POT®** slow cooker to LOW. Grease 2-quart soufflé dish or 2-pound coffee can; set aside. Beat granulated sugar and shortening in large bowl until blended. Add eggs, one at a time, mixing well after each addition.

Sift together flour, baking powder and salt. Add flour mixture and milk alternately to shortening mixture. Stir in chocolate chips and lemon peel.

Spoon batter into prepared dish. Cover with greased foil. Place in preheated **CROCK-POT®** slow cooker. Cook, covered, with slow cooker lid slightly ajar to allow excess moisture to escape, on LOW 3 to 4 hours or on HIGH 1 hour 45 minutes to 2 hours or until edges are golden and knife inserted into center of loaf comes out clean. Remove dish from **CROCK-POT®** slow cooker; remove foil. Place loaf on wire rack to cool completely.

Combine lemon juice and ¼ cup powdered sugar in small bowl until smooth. Add more sugar as needed to reach desired glaze consistency. Pour glaze over loaf. Drizzle loaf with melted chocolate.

TIP: To easily melt chocolate for a drizzle, place chocolate in a small microwavable container and heat for 60 seconds per ounce of chocolate. Chocolate may not appear melted, so stir it to determine if it has begun to soften.

chai tea cherries 'n cream

SERVINGS: 4 | PREP TIME: 10 MINUTES
HIGH: 2¼ HOURS

2   cans (15½ ounces each) pitted
     cherries in pear juice

2   cups water

½   cup orange juice

1   cup sugar

4   cardamom pods

2   cinnamon sticks (broken in half)

1   teaspoon grated orange peel

¼   ounce candied ginger, coarsely
     chopped

4   whole cloves

2   black peppercorns

4   green tea bags

1   container (6 ounces) fat-free
     black cherry yogurt

1   quart vanilla ice cream

     Mint sprigs (optional)

Drain cherries, reserving juice; set cherries aside. Combine reserved pear juice, water and orange juice in 4½-quart **CROCK-POT®** slow cooker. Mix in sugar, cardamom, cinnamon, orange peel, ginger, cloves and peppercorns. Cover; cook on HIGH 1¾ hours.

Remove spices with slotted spoon and discard. Stir in tea bags and reserved cherries. Cover; cook on HIGH 30 minutes.

Remove and discard tea bags. Remove cherries from liquid; set aside. Let liquid cool until warm. Whisk in yogurt until smooth.

To serve, divide warm cherries and yogurt sauce among 8 wide-rimmed wine or cocktail glasses or fancy bowls. Top each serving with small scoop of softened ice cream; swirl lightly. Garnish with mint.

poached autumn fruits with vanilla-citrus broth

SERVINGS: 4 TO 6 | PREP TIME: 15 MINUTES
HIGH: 2 HOURS

2   Granny Smith apples, peeled, cored and halved (reserve cores)

2   Bartlett pears, peeled, cored and halved (reserve cores)

1   orange, peeled and halved

5   tablespoons honey

1   vanilla bean, split and seeded (reserve seeds)

1   cinnamon stick

⅓   cup sugar

     Water

     Vanilla ice cream (optional)

Place apple and pear cores in 4½-quart **CROCK-POT®** slow cooker. Squeeze juice from orange halves into **CROCK-POT®** slow cooker. Add orange halves, honey, vanilla bean and seeds, cinnamon stick and sugar. Add apples and pears. Pour in enough water to cover fruit. Stir gently to combine. Cover; cook on HIGH 2 hours or until fruit is tender.

Remove apple and pear halves; set aside. Strain cooking liquid into large saucepan. Discard solids. Simmer gently over low heat until liquid reduces by half and thickens.

Dice apple and pear halves. Add to saucepan to rewarm fruit. To serve, spoon fruit with sauce into bowls. Top with vanilla ice cream.

peaches & cream mélange

2 tablespoons unsalted butter

¾ cup buttermilk baking mix

⅓ cup granulated sugar

¼ cup packed light brown sugar

2 eggs

2 teaspoons vanilla

2 cups fresh ripe peaches, pitted, peeled and mashed

1 cup light cream

1 tablespoon butter, melted

1 teaspoon ground cinnamon

1 teaspoon ground nutmeg

Coat 4½-quart **CROCK-POT®** slow cooker with 2 tablespoons butter. Combine baking mix, granulated sugar and brown sugar in large bowl. Add eggs and vanilla. Stir well to combine. Add peaches, cream, 1 tablespoon butter, cinnamon and nutmeg. Stir well to combine. Pour into **CROCK-POT®** slow cooker. Cover; cook on LOW 6 to 8 hours or on HIGH 3 to 4 hours.

brioche and amber rum custard

SERVINGS: 4 TO 6 **|** PREP TIME: 15 MINUTES
HIGH: 1¾ TO 2 HOURS **|** LOW: 3 TO 3½ HOURS

2	tablespoons unsalted butter
3½	cups heavy cream
4	large eggs
½	cup packed dark brown sugar
⅓	cup amber or light rum
2	teaspoons vanilla
1	loaf (20 to 22 ounces) brioche bread, torn into pieces or 5 large brioche, cut into thirds*
½	cup coarsely chopped pecans
	Caramel or butterscotch topping (optional)

***If desired, trim and discard heels.**

Generously coat 5- to 6-quart **CROCK-POT®** slow cooker with butter. Combine cream, eggs, brown sugar, rum and vanilla in large bowl. Stir well to combine.

Mound one-fourth of brioche pieces in bottom of prepared **CROCK-POT®** slow cooker. Ladle one-fourth of cream mixture over brioche. Sprinkle with one-third of pecans. Repeat layers with remaining brioche, cream mixture and nuts.

Cover; cook on LOW 3 to 3½ hours or on HIGH 1¾ to 2 hours. Continue cooking until custard is set and tester inserted into center comes out clean.

Serve warm. Drizzle with caramel or butterscotch topping.

chocolate malt pudding cake

SERVINGS: 6 TO 8 | PREP TIME: 15 MINUTES
HIGH: 2 TO 2½ HOURS

2 tablespoons unsalted butter

1 cup all-purpose flour

½ cup packed brown sugar

2 tablespoons unsweetened cocoa powder

1½ teaspoons baking powder

½ cup milk

2 tablespoons vegetable oil

½ teaspoon almond extract

½ cup coarsely chopped malted milk balls

½ cup semisweet chocolate chips

¾ cup granulated sugar

¼ cup malted milk powder

2 cups boiling water

4 ounces cream cheese, cubed, at room temperature

¼ cup sliced almonds (optional)

Vanilla ice cream (optional)

Generously butter 4½-quart **CROCK-POT®** slow cooker. Combine flour, brown sugar, cocoa powder and baking powder in medium bowl. Add milk, oil and almond extract. Stir until smooth.

Stir in malted milk balls and chocolate chips. Spread batter evenly in bottom of **CROCK-POT®** slow cooker.

Combine granulated sugar and malted milk powder in medium bowl. Mix boiling water and cream cheese in another bowl. Stir into malted milk mixture. Pour evenly over batter in **CROCK-POT®** slow cooker. Do not stir. Cover; cook on HIGH 2 to 2½ hours or until toothpick inserted in center comes out clean.

Let stand, uncovered, 30 minutes. Spoon into dessert dishes. Garnish with almonds and serve with ice cream.

spiked sponge cake

SERVINGS: 8 TO 10 | PREP TIME: 10 MINUTES
HIGH: 1½ TO 1¾ HOURS

CAKE

1   package (18.2 ounces) yellow cake mix

1   cup water

½   cup vegetable oil

4   large eggs

1   tablespoon grated orange peel

1   package (6 ounces) golden raisins and cherries or other chopped dried fruit (about 1 cup)

SAUCE

1   cup chopped pecans

½   cup sugar

½   cup (1 stick) butter

¼   cup bourbon or apple juice

Generously coat 5-quart **CROCK-POT®** slow cooker with nonstick cooking spray. Cut parchment paper to fit bottom. Press paper into **CROCK-POT®** slow cooker and spray lightly with nonstick cooking spray.

Combine cake mix, water, oil, and eggs in large bowl; stir well. (Batter may be lumpy). Stir in orange peel. Pour two-thirds of batter into **CROCK-POT®** slow cooker. Sprinkle dried fruits evenly over batter. Spoon on remaining batter evenly. Cover; cook on HIGH 1½ to 1¾ hours or until toothpick inserted into center of cake comes out clean.

Immediately remove stoneware from cooking base and cool 10 minutes on wire rack. Run flat rubber spatula around outer edges, lifting up bottom slightly. Invert onto serving plate. Peel off paper.

TO PREPARE SAUCE: Heat large skillet over medium-high heat until hot. Add pecans. Cook and stir 2 to 3 minutes or until pecans begin to brown. Add sugar, butter and bourbon and bring to a boil, stirring constantly. Cook 1 to 2 minutes longer or until sugar has dissolved. Pour sauce over entire cake or spoon sauce over each serving.

TIP: An easy way to fit parchment to **CROCK-POT®** slow cooker is to trace the bottom of the creamic insert onto parchment paper. Cut out and press in place as directed.

caramel & apple pound cake

SERVINGS: 6 TO 8 | PREP TIME: 20 MINUTES
HIGH: 4 TO 5 HOURS | LOW: 7 TO 9 HOURS

4	medium baking apples, cored, peeled and cut into wedges
½	cup apple juice
½	pound caramels, unwrapped
¼	cup creamy peanut butter
1½	teaspoons vanilla
½	teaspoon ground cinnamon
⅛	teaspoon ground cardamon
1	prepared pound cake, sliced

Coat inside of 4½-quart **CROCK-POT®** slow cooker with nonstick cooking spray. Layer apples, apple juice and caramels in **CROCK-POT®** slow cooker.

Mix together peanut butter, vanilla, cinnamon and cardamom in small bowl. Drop by teaspoons onto apples. Cover; cook on LOW 6 to 8 hours or on HIGH 3 to 4 hours.

Stir thoroughly and cook 1 hour longer. To serve, spoon warm apple mixture over cake slices.

pumpkin custard

2   eggs, beaten

1   cup solid-pack pumpkin

½   cup packed brown sugar

½   teaspoon ground ginger

½   teaspoon ground cinnamon,
     plus extra for garnish

½   teaspoon grated lemon peel

1   can (12 ounces) evaporated
     milk

Combine eggs, pumpkin, brown sugar, ginger, cinnamon and lemon peel in large bowl. Stir in evaporated milk. Pour mixture into 1½-quart soufflé dish. Cover tightly with foil.

Make foil handles (see note below). Place soufflé dish in 4½-quart **CROCK-POT®** slow cooker. Pour water into **CROCK-POT®** slow cooker to reach 1½ inches from top of soufflé dish. Cover; cook on LOW 4 hours.

Use foil handles to lift dish from **CROCK-POT®** slow cooker. Sprinkle with additional ground cinnamon. Serve warm.

Note: To make foil handles, tear off 3 (18×2-inch) strips of heavy-duty foil or use regular foil folded to double thickness. Crisscross foil strips in spoke design and place dish on center of strips. Pull foil strips up and over dish.

index

Mushrooms

Nuts

METRIC CONVERSION CHART

VOLUME MEASUREMENTS (dry)

$\frac{1}{8}$ teaspoon = 0.5 mL
$\frac{1}{4}$ teaspoon = 1 mL
$\frac{1}{2}$ teaspoon = 2 mL
$\frac{3}{4}$ teaspoon = 4 mL
1 teaspoon = 5 mL
1 tablespoon = 15 mL
2 tablespoons = 30 mL
$\frac{1}{4}$ cup = 60 mL
$\frac{1}{3}$ cup = 75 mL
$\frac{1}{2}$ cup = 125 mL
$\frac{2}{3}$ cup = 150 mL
$\frac{3}{4}$ cup = 175 mL
1 cup = 250 mL
2 cups = 1 pint = 500 mL
3 cups = 750 mL
4 cups = 1 quart = 1 L

VOLUME MEASUREMENTS (fluid)

1 fluid ounce (2 tablespoons) = 30 mL
4 fluid ounces ($\frac{1}{2}$ cup) = 125 mL
8 fluid ounces (1 cup) = 250 mL
12 fluid ounces (1$\frac{1}{2}$ cups) = 375 mL
16 fluid ounces (2 cups) = 500 mL

WEIGHTS (mass)

$\frac{1}{2}$ ounce = 15 g
1 ounce = 30 g
3 ounces = 90 g
4 ounces = 120 g
8 ounces = 225 g
10 ounces = 285 g
12 ounces = 360 g
16 ounces = 1 pound = 450 g

DIMENSIONS

$\frac{1}{16}$ inch = 2 mm
$\frac{1}{8}$ inch = 3 mm
$\frac{1}{4}$ inch = 6 mm
$\frac{1}{2}$ inch = 1.5 cm
$\frac{3}{4}$ inch = 2 cm
1 inch = 2.5 cm

OVEN TEMPERATURES

250°F = 120°C
275°F = 140°C
300°F = 150°C
325°F = 160°C
350°F = 180°C
375°F = 190°C
400°F = 200°C
425°F = 220°C
450°F = 230°C

BAKING PAN AND DISH EQUIVALENTS

Utensil	Size in Inches	Size in Centimeters	Volume	Metric Volume
Baking or Cake Pan (square or rectangular)	8×8×2	20×20×5	8 cups	2 L
	9×9×2	23×23×5	10 cups	2.5 L
	13×9×2	33×23×5	12 cups	3 L
Loaf Pan	8½×4½×2½	21×11×6	6 cups	1.5 L
	9×9×3	23×13×7	8 cups	2 L
Round Layer Cake Pan	8×1½	20×4	4 cups	1 L
	9×1½	23×4	5 cups	1.25 L
Pie Plate	8×1½	20×4	4 cups	1 L
	9×1½	23×4	5 cups	1.25 L
Baking Dish or Casserole			1 quart/4 cups	1 L
			1½ quart/6 cups	1.5 L
			2 quart/8 cups	2 L
			3 quart/12 cups	3 L